THE **5**

MISTAKES

EVERY INVESTOR MAKES

AND HOW TO

AVOID THEM

THE 5 MISTAKES

EVERY INVESTOR MAKES

AND HOW TO

AVOID THEM

Getting Investing **Right**

Second Edition

PETER MALLOUK

WILEY

For general information on our other products and services or for technical support, please contact our Customer Care Department within the United States at (800) 762-2974, outside the United States at (317) 572-3993, or fax (317) 572-4002.

Wiley publishes in a variety of print and electronic formats and by print-on-demand. Some material included with standard print versions of this book may not be included in e-books or in print-on-demand. If this book refers to media such as a CD or DVD that is not included in the version you purchased, you may download this material at http://booksupport.wiley.com. For more information about Wiley products, visit www.wiley.com.

Library of Congress Cataloging-in-Publication Data is Available:

ISBN 9781119794332 (hardback)
ISBN 9781119794356 (epdf)
ISBN 9781119794349 (epub)

Cover Design: Wiley
Cover Image: © djmilic/iStock/Getty Images

SKY10049676_062223

Contents

Preface

Over my career as a wealth manager, I have met thousands of individuals searching for a better way of investing. I noticed early on that most of the clients coming on board with my firm were terminating a prior advisor. It became clear to me that these clients weren't getting what they had hoped from their former advisors. While at times the issues were related to communication, relationships, and the like, sometimes the change was because the client wasn't getting the returns they had hoped, or their former advisor had blown up their portfolio. Mistakes had been made along the way.

Many investors don't enjoy investing, don't have the time for it, or don't feel they are particularly good at it. This type of investor searches for an advisor to alleviate the burden—to show them the way. Unfortunately, many if not most advisors make the same mistakes individuals often make. This is the tragedy of the financial services industry. As I have watched fortunes made, lost, and sometimes rebuilt again, I have observed the main problems that led to the deterioration of wealth. The conclusion is quite simple: *In most cases, if an investor has greatly underperformed from an investment perspective, it is not because of the markets, but because of their own, or their advisor's own, mistakes.* All of us, at times, are susceptible to at least one of these mistakes. Many of the greatest investors of all time acknowledge they have made them or are aware of them and actively put up mental roadblocks to prevent themselves from making them. For years, I have spoken about these mistakes, and this book will cover how to avoid these pitfalls and show a clear path toward achieving investment success.

Acknowledgments

This book wouldn't be possible without the ongoing efforts of Molly Rothove, Jessica Culpepper, James DeWitt, Brenna Stewart, and Jim Williams, all of whom contributed to this effort as well as to my newsletters, which are the constant source of in-house comedy prior to the editing process.

Special thanks to all of the incredibly talented people at Creative Planning, including those who helped with the research for the behavioral section of this book: Sarah Ayler, Andrew Horsman, Jeff Juday, Ashley Moulis, Meghan Perry, Conner Sivewright, Stacy Smith, and Chris Wolff.

A huge thank you to the clients of Creative Planning. I have learned so much from my clients over the years. Most importantly though, I learned that these are the type of people who make America what it is: the greatest place on earth to live. These folks make the economy go and grow and many of them have lived or are living the American Dream. My constant search for every possible way to help them has resulted in many of the things we do at my firm, and in the contents of this book.

To my mom who tricked me into believing I could do anything. I believed it until I was too old for it to matter. And to my dad, who taught me enough about investing at an early age that it became my passion. I especially cherish his advice to "ignore almost everything."

Thanks to my beautiful wife Veronica, who spent a lot of time driving on our family road trips while I worked on this book, and to my three wonderful kids Michael,[1] JP,[2] and Gabby[3] for always keeping me focused on the most important things in life. Finally, thank you to those who helped edit and shape this book. All errors are my own.

---

[1]He must have asked half a dozen times: "Is anyone going to read this book?"
[2]Thanks for updating me on the NCAA tournament scores while I was writing.
[3]Thanks for the hugs, delivered almost every hour on the hour!

About the Author

Peter Mallouk is the president of Creative Planning, named the #1 Independent Financial Advisory Firm in America by *Barron's* (2017). *Barron's* magazine named Peter the #1 Independent Financial Advisor in America three straight years (2013, 2014, and 2015). CNBC named Creative Planning the #1 Independent Wealth Management Firm in the United States (2014–2015). Peter is featured on both rankings of *Worth* magazine's Power 100, a list featuring the 100 most powerful men and women in global finance (2017, 2018). In 2017, Peter was a recipient of the Ernst & Young Central Midwest Entrepreneur of the Year Award. Creative Planning provides comprehensive wealth management services to high-net-worth clients, including investment management, financial planning, charitable planning, retirement plan consulting, tax planning, and estate planning services. Creative Planning currently manages over $70 billion for clients in all fifty states.

Legal Disclosure

Rankings and/or recognition by unaffiliated rating services and/or publications should not be construed by a client or prospective client as a guarantee that he/she will experience a certain level of results if Creative Planning (Company) is engaged, or continues to be engaged, to provide investment advisory services, nor should it be construed as a current or past endorsement of Company by any of its clients. Rankings published by magazines, and others, generally base their selections exclusively on information prepared and/or submitted by the recognized adviser. Rankings are generally limited to participating advisers. The Company never pays a fee to be considered for any ranking or recognition but may purchase plaques or reprints to publicize rankings. More information regarding rankings and/or accolades for Creative Planning can be found at:

http://www.creativeplanning.com/important-disclosure-information/

The Market Wants to Be Your Friend

Risk comes from not knowing what you are doing.

—Warren Buffett

You might be wondering why this book appears to be flipping you the bird right out of the box (see Figure I.1).[1] Well, that's the market for you. We often hear about the market averaging around 10 percent over long periods of time. That's true. It just doesn't do it in a nice, linear, stress-free way. It's all over the place. Let's check out the graph in Figure I.2 with the returns by year.

So, yes, it is true the market has averaged about a 10 percent return over the long run. However,

FIGURE I.1

---

[1]"Flipping the bird," otherwise known as "flipping you off" and a variety of other things, is a decidedly PG-13 concept. I am assuming you are 13 or that someone older than 17 gave you the book, and that this is not a concept you have never heard before or that you will take too much offense to. Besides, I'm not really flipping you the bird; the market is. I can't control that.

most investors never get anywhere near that return out of their stock invest-ments. The reason is that the market return varies. A lot. All the time. To be a successful investor, you need to get comfortable with this concept to avoid the mistakes all investors make or are tempted to make, whether it's market timing, actively trading stocks, falling prey to misleading performance data, behavioral mistakes, or not having a solid, disciplined plan.

So, what keeps investors from earning the market return? Quite simply, investors prevent themselves from participating in the returns the market wants to give them. *Investors go out of their way to make mistakes that keep them from getting the market return.*

FIGURE I.2

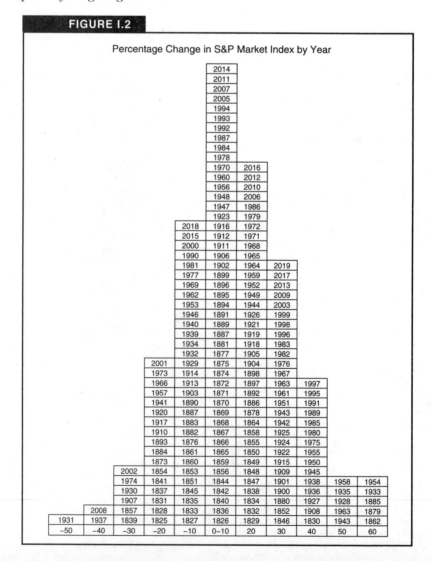

Percentage Change in S&P Market Index by Year

The first step to moving forward is to rid yourself of the misconceptions you may have about what works and become aware of the most common mistakes and avoid them. That's what this book is about. Recognizing the mistakes to avoid can dramatically improve your investment performance, reduce your stress level, substantially increase the probability you will achieve your investment goals, and even improve the quality of your life.

Let's begin.

THE 5
MISTAKES
EVERY INVESTOR MAKES
AND HOW TO
AVOID THEM

Market Timing

B oy, do I have an investment for you! It has earned about 10 percent per year over the last 88 years and has gone straight up. Check it out (see Figure 1.1)!

Now, what if I told you that return was real? More intriguing is that it is readily available to you. It's just waiting for you to participate. What is this incredible, magical investment? Well, it's something you may have heard of: the stock market.

If you are like most Americans, this sort of return seems like a dream. Numerous studies attempt to quantify the returns realized by individual investors relative to the market as a whole, and their conclusions are the same: Investors' stock portfolio returns regularly lag behind the stock market return and typically by a very wide margin. Market timing is the idea that there are times to be in the market and times to be out of it.

FIGURE 1.1

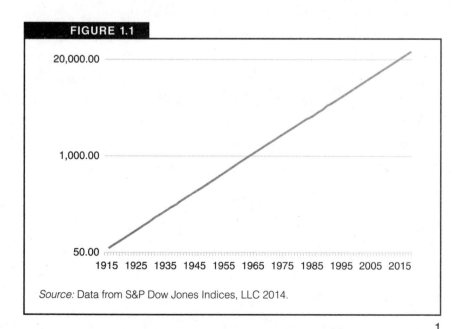

Source: Data from S&P Dow Jones Indices, LLC 2014.

Some people attempt to "protect" their money by exiting the market when they sense a downturn coming or load up on high-risk stocks when they anticipate a recovery.

Let's get one thing straight right out of the box. Market timing doesn't work. It just doesn't. And don't tell me you don't market time either. Have you ever said or thought anything like this:

> "I have cash on the sidelines, and I am just waiting for things to settle down."
>
> "I have a bonus, but I'll wait for a pullback."
>
> "I'll invest after [insert lame excuse here; some choices: the election, the new year, the market corrects, the debt crisis passes, Congress works out the budget, the Lions win the Super Bowl, or whatever]."

All of that is market timing.

Why would anyone want to get in the way of an investment that has perpetually produced such fantastical[1] returns?

Quite simply, it is because the stock market doesn't go up in a straight line. Drawn as the returns actually happened, the graph looks like the one shown in Figure 1.2.

That still doesn't look so bad when we look at it from here, with the full benefit of hindsight. Of course, living through it is an entirely different matter. Imagine the emotional turmoil you would have gone through during the Great Depression, the feeling of inertia and futility you would have had to endure through the 1970s, or the market panic during the early part of 2020 (actually, you likely don't need to imagine that one!). With investing, even a few weeks can seem like forever, especially when the market is moving against you.

To be clear, there are many "markets." The graphs we have looked at so far represent the Dow Jones Industrial Average, an index of 30 large

---

[1]Yes, it is a word! "Fantastic" didn't seem adequate enough to describe how great an investment stocks have been.

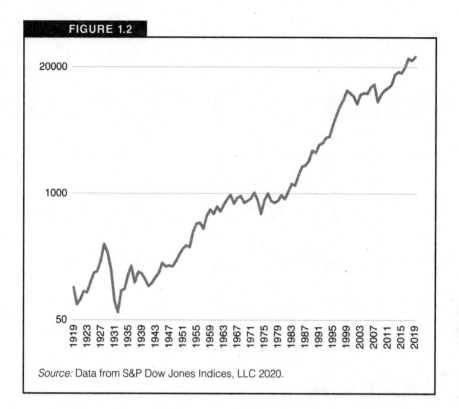

FIGURE 1.2

Source: Data from S&P Dow Jones Indices, LLC 2020.

U.S. companies with a history allowing us to go back more than 100 years. Today, the more common index is the S&P 500, an index of 500 large U.S. companies, like Microsoft, ExxonMobil, Google, Procter & Gamble, and Apple. While there are thousands of stocks, the largest 500 make up about 80 percent of the entire market. This is because companies like McDonald's, in the S&P 500, are hundreds of times larger than, say, the Cheesecake Factory.[2]

Just so no one thinks I am selecting the most awesomest[3] investment ever as an example, the same holds for small U.S. stocks, international

---

[2]Clearly, market capitalization is not a reflection on whose desserts are better. More on that later.

[3]Yes, I realize that this is actually not a word.

stocks, and emerging markets stocks. The point is that all broad markets have done the same thing: Go up—a lot.

All of this looks pretty good, right? But to get these returns, you need to avoid making the first big mistake: trying to "time the market." To avoid falling into this trap, it is critical to avoid the many people who are encouraging you to make this mistake: prognosticators on T.V., market timers, your buddy at work, your brother-in-law who "jumped out right before the last crash," and the majority of the financial services industry, to name a few.

This group of market timers can be divided into two camps, as illustrated in Figure 1.3.

Now, that chart isn't scientific. I don't really know what percentage of market timers are incompetent and what percentage are dishonest. However, I believe that market timers fall into one of these two camps, and both are dangerous. Let's take a look at both groups: the Idiots and the Liars.

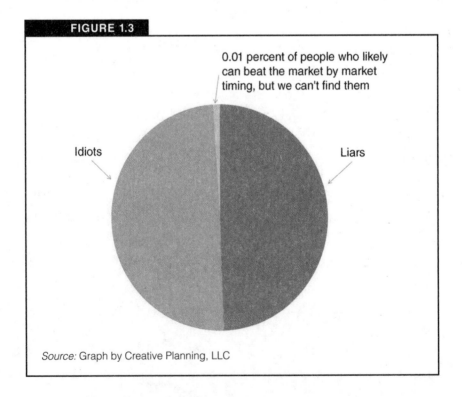

FIGURE 1.3

0.01 percent of people who likely can beat the market by market timing, but we can't find them

Idiots

Liars

Source: Graph by Creative Planning, LLC

The Idiots

What to do when the market goes down? Read the opinions of the investment gurus who are quoted in the WSJ. *And, as you read, laugh. We all know that the pundits can't predict short-term market movements. Yet there they are, desperately trying to sound intelligent when they really haven't got a clue.*

—Jonathan Clements

There are perfectly honest investors and advisors who believe they can time the market. They believe they know something that no one else knows or that they see something that no one else sees. They often will tell you they got it right before, and maybe they did—once. These folks are often like the friend of yours who tells you "I killed it, baby!" when he returns from Vegas, but conveniently leaves out the five times he lost. They forget their bad decisions and remember their good ones. They may be well-intentioned, but ultimately, they cause harm to their portfolios and to the portfolios of anyone who listens to them. These folks need to get educated and learn the folly of their ways. Luckily, you will soon be able to spot these people, avoid them, and maybe even save them from themselves.

The Liars

There are three kinds of people who make market predictions. Those who don't know, those who don't know what they don't know, and those who know darn well they don't know but get big bucks for pretending to know.

—Burton Malkiel[4]

Unfortunately, many financial advisors know very well that the market can't be timed, but their living depends on convincing you they can get you out with their "downside protection." This is the easiest sale in the financial advisory world. *There is nothing a prospective client wants to*

---

[4]Burton Malkiel wrote a revolutionary book on this subject called *A Random Walk Down Wall Street*. He is an advocate of using indexes at the core of a portfolio and active management in certain spaces "around the edges," a philosophy with which I agree.

hear more than the pitch that they can participate in the stock market's upward movement but avoid the pullbacks. There will always be people who want to hear this, and as long as those people exist, there will be tens of thousands of professionals ready to sell them snake oil.

I have also found that many financial advisors have been exposed to all the information they need to change their point of view away from market timing, but a big paycheck makes it hard to accept the facts. Much like a cult member finding definitive proof their founder is a fraud, the financial advisor can find the reality too much to accept and simply remain delusional and ignorant. As Descarte said, "Man is incapable of understanding any argument that interferes with his revenue."[5]

The prognosticators in the media also are eager to give you big, bold market calls. I have been on several national business channels, including CNBC and FOX Business. Prior to the show, the producer always asks me for my thoughts on "where the market is going." They are disappointed every time when I answer that over the short run, "I don't know." That doesn't make for the most exciting guest in the world. One national cable network even branded me "The Time Machine" advisor because I kept prefacing my advice by saying I had no idea what would happen in the short run but was very confident about the long run. The graphics were quite amusing, with my head sticking outside of a time machine that looked mainly like an old-school phone booth.[6]

In short, if you want to get clients and be on T.V., the easiest path is to sell market timing. The financial services industry rewards the deliberate delivery of misinformation.

Why Is It So Hard to Beat the Market?

In an efficient market, at any point in time, the actual price of a security will be a good estimate of its intrinsic value.

—Eugene Fama

---

[5]Also a very smart guy, but reading his books will teach you nothing about investing.

[6]My brother-in-law will never let me forget it.

There are many reasons market timing fails to work, and there are many reasons investment managers will try to tell you they can do it. Let's start by looking at the big picture, then work our way through the investment gurus and their actual results.

Efficient Markets

The efficient market hypothesis was developed by Nobel Laureate Eugene Fama. This investment theory can be summed up like this: It's tough to beat the market because markets are efficient at incorporating all relevant information. Since a bunch of smart people (and not so smart people) all know the same thing about any given security, it is impossible to have a sustainable edge that will allow you to beat the market return.

Where there appear to be patterns that the market can be beaten, it is almost always due to the investor taking on additional risk. For example, there is evidence that small company stocks perform better than large company stocks over long periods of time, and this is very likely because they are riskier (more volatile).

While it is not my point of view that the markets are perfectly efficient, the evidence is fairly overwhelming that it is efficient enough to kick a market timer's butt.[7] Regardless, it gives us a premise from which all the rest of the evidence will follow.

Being a Little Better Than the Market Isn't Good Enough

Why is it so difficult to go in and out of the market repeatedly with success? The problem is that many investors think you simply need to be right more than 50 percent of the time, when in fact, an exhaustive study by Nobel Laureate William Sharpe[8] definitively concluded that the investor must be right 69 to 91 percent of the time, depending on market moves (Sharpe 1975). Good luck with that.

---

[7]Technically speaking.

[8]Yes, at some point we will cite people who aren't Nobel Laureates.

The Evidence (Research and Stuff)

The evidence against market timing is overwhelming.

In what may be the most exhaustive study ever done on market timing, Richard Bauer and Julie Dahlquist examined over 1 million market timing sequences from 1926 to 1999. The conclusion: Holding the market outperformed over 80 percent of market timing strategies (Bauer and Dahlquist 2001, p. 38). That's a lot of scenarios run over a long period of time with one overwhelming conclusion. It doesn't seem to square with what many people do, what we hear from the masses, the media, economists, investment managers, newsletters, and your friends. Let's look at each.

The Masses Get It Wrong, Over and Over Again

We do not have an opinion about where the stock market, interest rates, or business activity will be a year from now. We've long felt the only value of stock forecasts is to make fortune-tellers look good. We believe that short-term market forecasts are poison and should be kept locked up in a safe place, away from children and also from grown-ups who behave in the market like children.

—Warren Buffett

For the average investor, there has been spectacular mistiming of the market. At the bottom of the coronavirus-fueled market meltdown in March 2020, investors obliterated records by pulling $326 billion from equities—more than triple the previous record from the 2008 financial crisis—and moving a record amount to cash. Within six months, the market had not only fully recovered but had moved into positive territory for the year. Investors had mistimed the market perfectly, breaking records both ways, both times at exactly the wrong time.

The Media Get It Wrong, Over and Over Again

The typical investor is getting their financial information from the media. It's important to note that the total sum value of all the information provided from the media regarding market calls is zero. Actually, it is less than zero because if you follow the guidance of the media on market calls, you are likely going to create a negative, rather than a neutral, result. Let's take a look at some examples:

"The Death of Equities." August 13th, 1979, *Businessweek*—just prior to the biggest stock market run-up in history.

"The Crash. . . . After a wild week on Wall Street, the world is different." November 11th, 1987, *Time*—the market proceeded to rocket 31 percent over the next 12 months.

"Buy Stocks. No Way!" September 26th, 1988, *Time*—just before the greatest 10-year run in market history.

"Will you be able to retire? With stocks plummeting and corporations in disarray, American's financial futures are in peril." July 29th, 2002, *Time*—the market was up 21 percent from July 2002 through June 2003.

The media's job is not to inform you; it is to get eyeballs. Eyeballs lead to advertising revenue. That means they need people to read stuff and view stuff. Telling everyone things are going to work out just fine doesn't get eyeballs the way feeding into fear does. That doesn't just explain financial news; it explains most of the news.

Economists Get It Wrong, Over and Over Again

If you are going to predict, predict often.

—John Kenneth Galbraith

Forecasts may tell you a great deal about the forecaster, but they tell you nothing about the future.

—Warren Buffett

He who predicts the future lies, even if he tells the truth.

—Proverbs

Economists have shown no ability to predict the direction of the economy. There are simply too many variables, many known and some unknown, for anyone to do so with any sort of sustainable accuracy. History provides us with two great anecdotes to this point. On October

15th, 1929, Irving Fisher, whom Milton Friedman declared the "greatest economist the United States has ever produced," asserted that "stock prices have reached what looks like a permanently high plateau." The following week, the market crashed, taking us into the Great Depression and beginning a free fall that would eventually see the Dow lose 88 percent of its value. It would be nearly 80 years before another stock market fall would come close to that one. Of course, there was a high profile economist making a bold prediction just prior to the turmoil. On January 10th, 2008, Ben Bernanke stated, "the Federal Reserve is currently not forecasting a recession."[9] Unfortunately, the economy didn't listen, as a few months later, the economy slid into the worst recession since the Great Depression, taking the stock market down more than 50 percent along the way.

Some economists have gained quite a bit of notoriety with their bold predictions. Bolder, it seems, is better. Harry Dent has become a quite popular economist despite his wildly unsuccessful market calls. It seems the more hyperbolic the predictions, the more attention he garners. In his 2006 book, *The Next Great Bubble Boom*, Dent wrote, "The Dow Jones Industrial Average could reach as high as 35,000 or 40,000 by late 2008 or 2009. . . . This continues to be our forecast. . . ." (Dent 2006, p. 44). Of course, we all know that the market fell into free fall in what turned out to be the greatest pullback since the Great Depression, bottoming in March of 2009. Almost stunning in its unfortunate timing, Dent came out with a new book in, you guessed it, 2009 called *The Great Depression Ahead* (Dent, 2008). In this book, Dent predicted that the recession would become a depression, and the Dow Jones Industrial Average would drop to 3,800. He strongly advocated that investors take any 2009 bounce in the market to sell all of their stocks and real estate and move to cash. This would be funny if it weren't so sad. Dent

---

[9]Now, ponder this for a moment. The Federal Reserve is arguably run by the best economic team on Earth. If they can't predict what is going to happen, and they control interest rates, which drive at least part of what happens, how are you, your buddy, or your financial guy going to predict what happens?

relentlessly promoted these books and was given a podium on financial networks to promote his forecasts. Both books were best sellers. Unfortunately, anyone following the "Boom" book went in at the wrong time, and much, much worse, anyone following the "Depression" book sold out at the worst possible time.

In advertisements in May 2013 on his *Survive & Prosper* website, Dent wrote, "I see the Dow Jones Average winding down, week after week . . . before ultimately dropping as low as 3,300. And there's nothing you or I, or any politician or government, or any team of monetary experts can do to stop the Dow Jones Index from dropping. . . . But here's the good news, extraordinary wealth can be made by knowing the future. In *Survive & Prosper*, my free e-letter, I'll show you my economic analysis and demographic research that proves the DOW is about to make a historic drop. I will show how predicting and profiting from the future is a SCIENCE and is easier than you might have imagined" (Dent 2013). This guy, like just about everyone selling their ability to time the market, is nothing but a charlatan.

Despite making spectacularly wrong prediction after spectacularly wrong prediction, AIM partnered with him to start a mutual fund tracking his advice, the "AIM Dent Demographic Trends Fund." It quickly gathered $2 billion in assets, largely due to the publicity that surrounds Dent. It quickly lost 80 percent of its assets due to terrible performance. Dent said it was due to the fund not taking all of his advice. Dent may have a harder time explaining the performance of the "Dent ETF," which was launched on September 9th, 2009, and was run by "HS Dent Investment Management" until they resigned on June 2nd, 2012. On his website, Dent calls his methodology ". . . real-time insights and analysis that helps [people] . . . make profitable decisions." So how did the ETF perform while he managed it? During their tenure, it lost 12.9 percent. Over the same time period, the U.S. market was up 42.7 percent, and the bond market was up 18.2 percent. It is very difficult to lose this much money during a bull market. It's almost impossible to do, even if you try. Despite being so wrong so many times, Dent still has his followers and gets plenty of media airplay. Extreme predictions have no problem finding airwaves.

Most economists cannot forecast the market correctly, and the evidence bears that out. However, occasionally, an economist does make what appears to be an accurate forecast. One such economist is the now-famous Dr. Nouriel Roubini, the Chairman of Roubini Global Economics. Roubini, now known as the ominous "Dr. Doom,"[10] warned the public about the coming recession prior to it occurring. However, according to the Economic Predictions Research Project as published on the Wall Street Economists Institute website, Dr. Doom actually predicted a recession in 2004 (incorrectly), 2005 (oops, no recession), 2006 (sorry, still no recession), and 2007 (you guessed it, still no recession). If you followed Dr. Doom's advice, yes, you would have been out of the market prior to the 2008 drop, but you also would have been out of it for the four years prior and a few years after. All in all, you would have far less money following Dr. Doom's predictions than had you done nothing!

At an International Monetary Fund meeting in 2006, Dr. Doom was quoted as saying:

> My analysis has been based on circumstantial kind of observations . . . I said the probability of a recession is "70 percent." If you ask me where I got that number: just out of my nose.[11] I will be very honest about that. I think if you would have said "50 percent," you would look like a wimp; it means you are not sure. So if you have the guts of believing there is going to be a recession, you should say something higher than that, and that is where the "70 percent" comes from. So my model is like a "smell test."

Translation: Dr. Doom, perhaps the most celebrated economic forecaster of the time, is basically saying his guesses are based on a "smell test," and he inflates his hunches to appear more confident.

---

[10]You have officially hit it big as an economist when you have a nickname. Dr. Roubini is Dr. Doom. March Faber, another high-profile doomsday permabear, also has a nickname. It's also Dr. Doom. It seems that the longer and louder you are about how bad things are about to get, the more likely you will get a nickname, albeit not an original one.

[11]My personal opinion is that he got it right out of somewhere else.

I can't make this stuff up. Seriously!

Again, it would be funny if the financial media didn't elevate him and let his opinions about market movements carry such weight and go unchallenged. If a viewer saw Dr. Doom explain his outlook while the financial network showed his former predictions alongside a running ticker, perhaps he wouldn't carry quite the weight he does, and instead elicit an eye roll. Unfortunately, all people hear is that Dr. Doom predicted the 2008 recession and then listen carefully, and often act upon, his newer, ominous (as is almost always the case) predictions.

Now, I know what you're thinking: "Well, Dr. Doom might be the most famous economist to predict the crisis, but his failure to correctly predict almost anything else isn't indicative of economic forecasters in general."[12] Well, thanks for bringing that point up. Let's take a look at the entire field of economic forecasters who, like Harry Dent and Dr. Doom, make strong predictions.

Fortunately, I don't need to spend time researching to figure this out. Oxford economist Jerker Denrell and Christina Fang of New York University looked at all the predictions in the *Wall Street Journal*'s Survey of Economic Forecasts from July 2002 through July 2005 (Denrell and Fang 2010). They then narrowed their search to isolate the group of economists who had proven to be the most successful at predicting unlikely outcomes. To do this, they defined an "extreme" prediction as one in which the economist's outlook was either 20 percent higher or 20 percent lower than the average prediction. Now, these economists appear to be darn good at predicting things. After all, they are taking positions where they stand alone, or in the minority, and have been proven right.

Well, not so much. Denrell and Fang then looked at the other predictions of this group and found that these economists, the ones with the best success rate at predicting "extreme" events, actually had a *worse* record overall. In other words, the crazier the prediction an economist

---

[12]Or you could be thinking, "It's time for a sandwich break." Hey, I'm not a mind reader!

makes, the more likely he is to hit a home run every now and then, but the more likely he is to strike out far more than normal. Is this the type of person you want to get investment advice from?

Here's the deal: The more certain a forecaster is of their prediction, the less likely they are to be right, and the more likely their prediction is a derivative of showmanship. When it comes to investing, the bolder the prediction, the less valid the source. If you care about your financial well-being, the data strongly suggests you would be far better off ignoring it. Joe Stiglitz, a Nobel Prize-winning economist,[13] has said that economists get it right "about 3 or 4 times out of 10" (Weber 2011). With those odds, I'll pass. You should too.

Investment Managers Get It Wrong, Over and Over Again

Sure, it would be great to get out of the stock market at the high and back in at the low, but in 55 years in the business, I not only have never met anybody that knew how to do it, I've never met anybody who had met anybody that knew how to do it.

—John Bogle, founder of Vanguard

There are literally thousands, if not tens of thousands, of financial advisors claiming to have "market indicators" that help them time the market. The most well-known among this group is Ken Fisher. Ken runs one of the largest investment management firms in America and was a popular *Forbes* columnist from 1984 to 2017. He believes that his firm can ". . . interpret information differently and find global investing opportunities other money managers may overlook," which is ". . . the best way to . . . achieve long-term results," according to Fisher Investments' website. While Ken uses direct marketing and a legion of marketing representatives to promote his private portfolio management service, they rarely mention the publicly available mutual fund they used to run. The Purisima Total Return Fund (PURIX) consisted of securities chosen by Ken and his team, presumably following his tried-and-tested

---

[13]Here we go again with the Nobel Prize guys.

strategy for success, from 1996 up until he decided to close the fund in 2016. According to Gurufocus, the fund managed to underperform the S&P 500 across every meaningful time frame, and not just by a little bit: the cumulative relative underperformance for 3, 5, 10, and 15 years were eye-popping at −20.71%, −51.11%, −52.86%, and −16.00%, respectively (Gurufocus.com 2020).

In September 2007, Ken wrote in his column: "This is a phony credit crunch . . . a few months from now we will be wondering what the fuss was about" (Fisher, 2007). Perhaps Ken's boldest prediction came in January 2008, as the market began its downward spiral. Ken wrote in his column: "Let me make you a solemn promise for 2008 . . . America should do well in 2008—better, at any rate, than people expect. My advice is to stay fully invested on a global basis, with stocks like these." (Fisher, 2008).

Of course, what followed was the biggest single calendar year loss the stock market had seen since the Great Depression, and in 2008 the Purisima Fund run by Fisher's team was down 42.95 percent, far worse than the S&P 500.

Let's be clear, though—while Ken Fisher is one of the biggest market timers, he is not alone in his inability to consistently time the market correctly, or even enough to outperform. As Don Phillips, the managing director of Morningstar, said: "I can't point to any mutual fund anywhere in the world that's produced a superior long-term record using market timing as its main investment criteria" (Britton 2011).

While Ken Fisher was wrong about 2008, Peter Schiff nailed it. As early as December of 2006, investment advisor Peter Schiff predicted the coming economic crisis. However, the Economic Predictions Research Project, as published on the Wall Street Economists Institute website, puts that in context. Below is a list of Peter Schiff's major predictions from 2002 through 2012:

May 2002—The DOW will drop to 4,000—DID NOT HAPPEN.

December 16th, 2006—Interest rates and inflation will go higher—
    DID NOT HAPPEN.

December 16th, 2006—There will be inflation in 2008 and 2009—
    DID NOT HAPPEN.

December 16th, 2006—U.S. equities will crash—HAPPENED! This is
the prediction he is known for getting "right."

Predicted repeatedly prior to and during the crisis: Buy foreign
equities and commodities—DID NOT HAPPEN and a big "oops." It
turns out that while he was right about the U.S. market, his solution was
not so right. Foreign equities actually sold off far more than U.S. stocks,
down over 43 percent. Peter Schiff invested his clients per his recommendations, and they sustained the brunt of the crash.

January 16th, 2009—At a minimum, the dollar will lose another
   40 to 50 percent in 2010—DID NOT HAPPEN.

January 2nd, 2009—U.S. stocks are heading a lot lower in 2009, 2010,
   and 2011.—DID NOT HAPPEN—over this time period, U.S.
   stocks were up approximately over 40 percent!

September 9th, 2009—Gold will go to $5,000—DID NOT HAPPEN.

September 9th, 2009—U.S. dollar will go close to zero—DID
   NOT HAPPEN.

January 12th, 2010—Buy commodities like gold—HAPPENED,
   except they later crashed with his clients still in the asset class.

August 26th, 2010—We probably won't make it to 2012—DID
   NOT HAPPEN.

December 31st, 2010—U.S. markets will crash like dominos, and many
   bad things are bound to happen in 2011—DID NOT HAPPEN.

To sum it up, Peter Schiff did make a major market prediction, *but*
his solution didn't work, and most of his other predictions have been
dead wrong. I concur with Todd Sullivan of Seeking Alpha, who wrote:
"had you placed bets on Schiff's market calls, you lost everything you
wagered" (Sullivan 2008).

The bottom line is this: There are tens of thousands of investment
managers who claim to be able to market time. Some are famous, and
some are not. They all have one thing in common, though: None of
them can do this effectively and repeatedly. The odds of getting it right

over time are extremely low, and only a fool would play such a game with the markets. An even bigger fool would pay someone else to gamble with their money this way. The odds are so stacked against the market timer that any long-term outcome other than colossal failure is rarely avoidable.[14]

Newsletters Get It Wrong, Over and Over Again

The only way to make money with a newsletter is by selling one.

—Malcolm Forbes

Tens of thousands of Americans subscribe to a variety of market timing newsletters. These Americans are paying a fee and spending a lot of time to increase their chances of underperforming the market.

In 1994, John Graham and Campbell Harvey, analyzing data provided by Mark Hulbert,[15] conducted what many consider the most comprehensive study on the ability of newsletters to predict the market (Graham and Harvey 1994). They looked at over 15,000 market timing calls from 237 newsletters over 13 years. The conclusion was overwhelming: 75 percent of the newsletters produced negative abnormal returns. Basically, following the advice of most of these letters created negative performance!

Some of the newsletters, like the once-famous *Granville Market Letter*, produced an average negative annual return of 5.4 percent. The *Elliot Wave Theorist* letter, a favorite of doomsday fanatics, produced a negative annual return of 14.8 percent.[16] During the same time period, the S&P 500 earned 15.9 percent per year, outperforming a full three-quarters of the newsletters.

---

[14]Rule #1 of investing: Avoid colossal failure. Colossal failure is bad.

[15]Mark Hulbert runs a service that tracks newsletter predictions and performance.

[16]Isn't it interesting how the doomsday fanatics end up losing their money despite their desperate attempts to save it?

You might ask, well, what about the one-quarter that did match or beat the market? It seems impossible, but the study actually overstates the performance of market timing newsletters. Had the study accounted for fees, transaction costs, and taxes, the underperformance would have been even worse! Finally, the authors took their study further, checking to see if winners keep on winning. The conclusion is clear: "Winners rarely win again."

The authors are harsh and definitive in the conclusion of their study, saying, "There is no evidence that the letters can time the market."

Mark Hulbert's own research shows that the few that do outperform the market in any given year are not the same in future years (Snider 2014). In other words, a good year has no predictive value looking forward. His data on market timing letters specifically provides an even more dismal outlook: His data shows that not a single market timing newsletter has beaten the market over the long run (Snider 2014)!

Your Buddy

Only liars manage to always be out during bad times and in during good times.
—Bernard Baruch

Of course, we all know that one guy—the one who "had a feeling" about when to get out of the market.[17] He is like your buddy who tells you about the times he won in Vegas but forgets to include all the times he lost. There is no doubt that some people get some market calls right. There will always be people who do. However, to be successful, they need to be right about when to get out *and* when to move back into the market. More importantly, they need to do this *repeatedly*. In all likelihood, the person who got it right this time has tried it many times in the past and will continue to do so in the future. *The odds are incredibly high that this person will ultimately fail.* In my entire career, I have personally

---

[17]Your buddy says stuff like this: "Dude, the market is so overvalued. Anyone can see that!" or "The charts made it so easy to know when to get out before the last correction."

never seen an investor exit the market near a top and enter it again near a bottom. Not once. And whoever does do it needs to do it over and over to succeed. Do you really think your buddy can do something even the pros can't do? The statistics, the probabilities, and not to mention plain old common sense, say no.

Strategies That Don't Sound Like Market Timing but Are Market Timing—Oh, and They Don't Work Either

If you are ever talking with an advisor who tells you he doesn't market time, ask further questions. They will often try to sell you what you want to hear, which is market timing packaged differently. If you hear terms like "downside protection," "asset-class rotation," "tactical allocation," "style rotation," and "sector rotation," they are implying that they can regularly predict when to move from one part of the market to another. All of this is market timing—and the evidence is overwhelming that it does not work.

Asset-Class Rotation

An asset-class rotation strategy attempts to select the ideal time to move from one asset class to another. The "sale" here is usually "downside protection." When marketed, advisors often sell the idea they will own stocks while the market is going up but will shift to cash before it goes down. In his 1984 article, "The Folly of Stock Market Timing," Robert Jeffrey examined annual switches between stocks and cash. He concluded, "the potential downside from market timing exceeds the potential upside by a wide margin" (Jeffrey 1984). Any time you hear "asset-class rotation" or "downside protection strategy," your BS meter should be beeping loudly.[18]

---

[18]If you haven't noticed, part of being successful at investing is having a really good BS meter. We are talking really advanced. Off the shelf won't do it. There's just too much BS out there to survive without anything but the best.

Tactical Asset Allocation

Tactical asset allocation funds attempt to beat the market by moving from one broad asset class to another. In February 2012, Morningstar compared 210 tactical asset allocation portfolios against a 60 percent stock/40 percent bond Vanguard portfolio. The conclusion: "With a few exceptions, they gained less, were more volatile, or were subject to just as much downside risk as a 60 percent/40 percent mix of U.S. stocks and bonds" (Ptak 2012). In other words, tactical allocation provides a wilder ride for a lower return.[19] No, thank you!

Style Rotation

With this strategy, an advisor is selling the idea they can move from one investing style to another at optimal times. Typical style rotation strategies include moving from value stocks to growth stocks or attempting to move from large dividend-paying stocks to small stocks at the right times. Same deal—the evidence supports that this doesn't work.

Sector Rotation

A sector rotation strategy promises outperformance by moving from one sector to another at the right time. For example, a money manager may move from financial stocks to health care stocks, depending on where they see the economy going. Again, this is just market timing under another name, and the evidence indicates that this doesn't work either.

What Smart Investors Have to Say on Market Timing

The market timing Hall of Fame is an empty room.

—Jane Bryant Quinn

---

[19]The irony of these strategies is that they often create more volatility and deliver a lower return, which is the exact opposite of what the investor is attempting to accomplish.

Among the great investors of all time, none of them advocate market timing. J. P. Morgan, who dominated finance in his time, was asked by a young investor what the market would do. J. P. Morgan replied, "It will fluctuate, young man. It will fluctuate." Benjamin Graham, the father of modern investing, advocated against market timing, saying in 1976, "If I have learned anything over these 60 years on Wall Street, it is that people do not succeed in forecasting what is going to happen in the stock market." John Bogle, the founder of Vanguard, the largest fund company in the world, has repeatedly said that he finds market timing impossible and futile. Warren Buffett, who has been peerless in modern-day investing, has mocked market timing repeatedly, often citing it as the stupidest thing an investor can do. He has many thoughts on the subject, including "Forecasters exist to make fortune-tellers look good" and, more to the point, "I have *never* met a man that can time the market."

Knowing All This, Why Would Anyone Market Time?

Wall Street never changes, the pockets change, the suckers change, the stocks change, but Wall Street never changes, because human nature never changes.
—Jesse Livermore

Knowing that media, economists, newsletters, investment managers, and just about everyone else have not successfully timed the market, and having seen what legendary investors have to say about market timing, why would anyone try to use market timing? Reasons for both the investor and "professional" selling market timing are the same: ignorance, greed, or both. Investors want to believe someone can get in before the market goes up and get out before it goes down. None of the other investment strategies sound nearly as appealing, even if they can lessen losses or increase gains. And if people want it, someone will sell it and keep a straight face while doing so. To make it easier to sneak by you, the advisor may not call it market timing but instead use code for market timing. Upton Sinclair once said: "It is difficult to get a man to understand something when his salary depends on not understanding it." For as long as we are alive, there will be thousands of advisors selling market timing. You can count on it!

To survive market turmoil without getting pulled into the market-timing mistake, one must understand the frequency of significant market moves, especially corrections and bear markets.

Corrections

Far more money has been lost by investors preparing for corrections, or trying to anticipate corrections, than has been lost in corrections themselves.

—Peter Lynch

A stock market correction is coming. Guaranteed.

That is quite a statement since I just spent a few thousand words talking about how market timing is practically impossible. So, how can I make such a prediction? I can make it because stock market corrections happen all the time. They are a given. Predicting one is like saying, "It is going to rain sometime this year."

Let us start with the definition of a "correction." It is simply a stock market drop of 10 percent or more. If the market drops a total of 20 percent, we change the name from correction to "bear market."

How frequently does a correction occur? Using the year 1900 as a starting point, history tells us that corrections happen approximately every year. So if you are around age 55 and reading this, you should plan on experiencing about 30 or more corrections.

Why not get out of the market once it drops 10 percent to avoid a further drop into bear market territory? The reason is that most corrections never officially become bear markets. Historically, the average correction is a drop of 13.7 percent. Most corrections last less than two months, with the average length of a correction sitting at just around four months. Less than one in five corrections turns into an official bear market.

Knowing this, it does not make sense to go to cash whenever a correction occurs. In fact, with odds like that, it is an illogical decision to convert to cash once the market drops 10 percent. You would be moving to cash right before the typical bottom. Imagine how badly you could screw up your portfolio if you reacted this way to even a few of these corrections!

Predicting stock market corrections and bear markets is a sport of sorts. To make matters more difficult, sometimes corrections happen for a reason, and sometimes they do not.

We know it is a fact that corrections happen all the time. We know that most corrections do not evolve into bear markets. We also know that every single correction in history has given way to a full recovery. It seems utterly ridiculous to panic and move to cash. The math is against you, the evidence is against you, and the market's natural bias is against you—all three are going to get together and do severe damage to your portfolio. It is fun, however, to watch market prognosticators make themselves look spectacularly silly predicting a correction. Figure 1.4 shows just a small sampling of predictions from the pros during a recent two-year period—the market refused to correct for them, despite their confident proclamations. Enjoy.

The following are some corresponding market prognosticators' correction predictions from Figure 1.4:

1. "Market Correction Ahead," Bert Dohmen, Dohmen Capital Research Group, March 7th, 2012

2. "Stocks Flirt with Correction," Ben Rooney, *CNNMoney*, June 1st, 2012

3. "10 Percent Market Correction Looms: Dig In or Bail Out?" Matt Krantz, *USA Today*, June 5th, 2012

4. "A Significant Equity-Price Correction Could, in Fact, Be the Force That in 2013 Tips the U.S. Economy into Outright Contraction," Nouriel Roubini, Roubini Global Economics, July 20th, 2012

5. "Prepare for Stock Market Crash 2013," Jonathan Yates, moneymorning.com, July 23rd, 2012

6. "Dr. Doom 2013 Prediction: Roubini Says Worse Global Economic Turmoil Approaching; Five Factors to Blame," Kukil Bora, *International Business Times*, July 24th, 2012

7. "Watch Out for a Correction—or Worse," Mark Hulbert, MarketWatch, August 8th, 2012

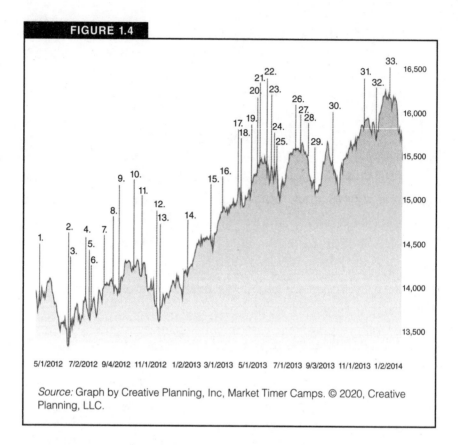

FIGURE 1.4

Source: Graph by Creative Planning, Inc, Market Timer Camps. © 2020, Creative Planning, LLC.

8. "We think we are set up for an 8–10 percent correction in the month of September," MaryAnn Bartels, Bank of America Merrill Lynch, August 22nd, 2012

9. "It's Coming: One Pro Sees Big Stock Selloff in 10 Days," John Melloy, CNBC, September 4th, 2012

10. "Warning: Stock Correction May Be Coming," Hibah Yousuf, *CNNMoney*, October 4th, 2012

11. "I'm going around town telling my hedge fund clients that the U.S. economy is headed into recession," Michael Belkin, Belkin Limited, October 15th, 2012

12. "Fiscal Cliff Blues May Lead to Correction," Caroline Valetkevitch and Ryan Vlastelica, Reuters, November 9th, 2012

13. "Why a Severe Stock Market Correction's Imminent," Mitchell Clark, Lombardi Financial, November 14th, 2012

14. "By summer, we get another crash," Harry Dent, Dent Research, January 8th, 2013

15. "A Stock Market Correction May Have Begun," Rick Newman, *U.S. News*, February 21st, 2013

16. "Sluggish Economy May Signal Correction," Maureen Farrell, CNNMoney.com, February 28th, 2013

17. "I think a correction is coming," Byron Wein, Blackstone, April 4th, 2013

18. "Market's Long Overdue Correction Seems to Be Starting," Jonathan Castle, Paragon Wealth Strategies, April 8th, 2013

19. "5 Warning Signs of a Coming Market Correction," Dawn Bennett, Bennett Group Financial Services, April 16th, 2013

20. "Stock Market Warning Signs Becoming Ominous," Sy Harding, StreetSmartReport.com, April 22nd, 2013

21. "Don't buy—sell risk assets," Bill Gross, PIMCO, May 2nd, 2013

22. "This may not be the time to sprint away from risk, but it is the time to walk away," Mohamed El-Erian, PIMCO, May 22nd, 2013

23. "We're due for a correction soon," Byron Wein, Blackstone, June 3rd, 2013

24. "Doomsday Poll: 87 Percent Risk of Stock Crash by Year-End," Paul Farrell, MarketWatch, June 5th, 2013

25. "Stock Shrink: Market Heading for Severe Correction," Adam Shell, *USA Today*, June 15th, 2013

26. "Don't Be Complacent—A Market Correction Is On Its Way," Sasha Cekerevac, Investment Contrarians, July 12th, 2013

27. "For Two Months, My Models Have Told Me That July 19th Would be the start of a Big Stock Market Sell-Off," Jeff Saut, Raymond James, July 18th, 2013

28. "Signs of a Market Correction Ahead," John Kimelman, *Barron's*, August 13th, 2013

29. "Correction Watch: How Soon? How Bad? How to Prepare?" Kevin Cook, Zacks.com, August 23rd, 2013

30. "I Think There's a Decent Chance Stocks Will Crash," Henry Blodget, *Business Insider*, September 26th, 2013

31. "5 Reasons to Expect a Correction," Jeff Reeves, MarketWatch, November 18th, 2013

32. "Time to Brace for a 20 Percent Correction," Richard Rescigno, *Barron's*, December 14th, 2013

33. "Blackstone's Wien: Stock Market Poised for 10 Percent Correction," Dan Weil, Moneynews.com, January 16th, 2014

Bear Markets: An Overview

The key to making money in equities is to not get scared out of them.
—Peter Lynch

A bear market is coming. Guaranteed.

I know, I know. I just said that about corrections. Well, it's true about bear markets too. Bear markets don't happen nearly as frequently as corrections, but they also happen all the time. A bear market is defined as a stock market decline of 20 percent or more.[20] Bear markets occur every three to five years, depending on how far back in history you want to look. There have been 35 bear markets from 1900 to 2020, including 15 since 1946. The four bear markets from 2000 on have been jarring for investors with all sorts of crises assaulting the markets. The average bear market decline is 31 percent, and more than one-third of bear markets have suffered drops of over 40 percent. The average bear market lasts close to a year; almost all last between eight months and two years.

---

[20] 10 percent and 20 percent are just numbers, but in real life, when experienced, they elicit quite different reactions. If a correction feels unsettling to you, a bear market will make you want to curl up in a ball and cry for Mommy.

Figure 1.5		

BEAR MARKETS: HOW OFTEN, HOW LONG, AND HOW SEVERE?

YEAR(S)	NUMBER OF DAYS IN LENGTH	% DECLINE IN S&P 500
1946–1947	353	−23.2%
1956–1957	564	−19.4%
1961–1962	195	−27.1%
1966	240	−25.2%
1968–1970	543	−35.9%
1973–1974	694	−45.1%
1976–1978	525	−26.6%
1981–1982	472	−24.1%
1987	101	−33.5%
1990	87	−21.2%
1998	45	−19.3%
2000–2001	546	−36.8%
2002	200	−32.0%
2007–2009	515	−57.6%
2020	33	−33.9%

The most recent bear market was the shortest on record at 33 days (see Figure 1.5).

Bear Markets Happen for Different Reasons, but the Outcome Is Always the Same

The four most expensive words in the English language are: "This time it's different."

—John Templeton

Bear markets occur when many people think things are going to be bad for a long time. If we know that every bear market has given way to a bull market, why would anyone ever panic and go to cash? The reason is that each bear market tends to happen for a different reason than the one before it. Looking at recent bear markets, we have everything from a tech bubble to a terrorist event and war, a liquidity crisis, and a global pandemic. Because each drop is driven by a different set of facts, investors panic, thinking that "this time is different." While the actual set of facts driving the bear market may be different, the outcome is always the same: The economy finds a way to move on. Every single time. No exceptions! The next time we go through a bear market, remind yourself of all the things we have been through in the past 80 years. If the economy can survive all of this, it can likely get through the next bear market:

1940s World War II

1960s/1970s Vietnam War

1970/1980s Hyperinflation

1970s/1980s Commodity Crisis

1980s Real Estate and Banking Collapse

1980s Emerging Markets Crisis

1987 Flash Crash

1990s Asian Contagion Crisis

2000 Tech Bubble Bursts

2001 9/11 Attack and Subsequent Afghanistan and Iraq Wars

2008/2009 Liquidity Crisis

2020 Coronavirus Pandemic

Figure 1.6 shows what it looks like against the market.

And keep in mind that the previous list is by no means all-inclusive. There are many distractions along the way that will cause prognosticators to predict the next bear, whether it is a downgrade of the United States, a "fiscal cliff," a budget debate, an election, or whatever happens to be the news cycle of the day.

Bear Markets Are Not Predictable

Here's the thing, though: Bear markets are not predictable. No one on earth has consistently and repeatedly predicted bear markets. Remember,

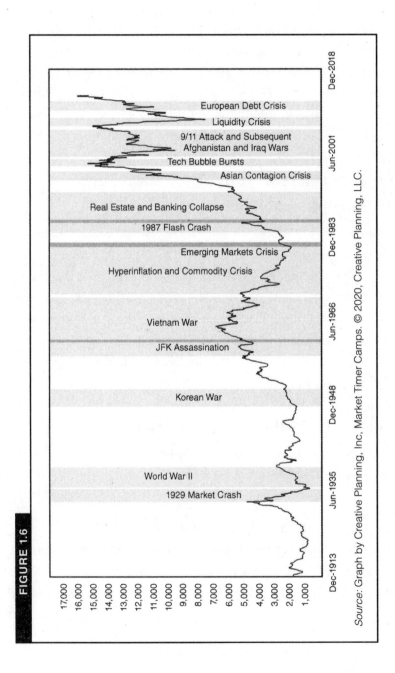

FIGURE 1.6

Source: Graph by Creative Planning, Inc, Market Timer Camps. © 2020, Creative Planning, LLC.

to exploit a bear market, you need to know when to get out, know when to get back in, and then do it again. I can't find the person who's done that. You're not going to find them either. Like Santa Claus, you might want to think he exists, for a while you believe he exists, there comes the point where you know enough to know he doesn't exist, but you can't admit it yourself, and then finally, maybe you will accept it. Also, like Santa Claus, there are a lot of people running around pretending to be that guy you want to believe in so badly.[21]

When Bear Markets "Turn," They Make People on the Sidelines Look Silly

Now, you might acknowledge that you can't possibly get out and back correctly and repeatedly, but you may be thinking: "I'll at least get out and wait for things to settle, miss a small part of the recovery, then jump back in." To do so is likely not possible. When bear markets give way to bull markets, they often first have several false starts, but when they "turn" for real, *they tend to do so quickly and furiously*, leaving most market timers sitting with their hands firmly under their derrières. Figure 1.7 illustrates this point.

The Market Is Volatile—Get Used to It

You get recessions. You get market declines. If you don't understand that it is going to happen, then you won't do well in the markets.

—Peter Lynch

Sometimes a year goes by without a correction or bear market. Sometimes the market ends the year with a solid return, and in the rear-view mirror, it looks easy. That is very rarely the case—*the market trades in broad ranges*. Since 1980, the market has had an average intra-year decline

---

[21]I'm pretty sure that with the book's opening graph, I eliminated the chance of anyone reading this book who still believes in Santa Claus.

Figure 1.7	
BEAR MARKET BOTTOM	**NEXT 12 MONTHS (S&P 500)**
6/13/1949	42.1%
10/22/1957	31.0%
6/26/1962	32.7%
5/26/1970	43.7%
10/3/1974	38.0%
8/12/1982	59.4%
12/4/1987	22.4%
9/21/2001	−12.5%
7/23/2002	17.9%
3/9/2009	69.5
3/23/2020	N/A

of 13.8 percent *but still had positive annual returns for 30 of the past 40 years!* (See Figure 1.8.) The market moves around a lot. Accept it, embrace it, learn to love it. If you can't do that, well then, at least get used to it!

You Can't Wait for Consumers to Feel Good

Bull markets are born on pessimism.

—John Templeton

You not only can't wait for things to "settle," you also can't use consumer confidence as an indicator. You might notice that during bear markets, commentators often talk a lot about "consumer confidence." They do this because the consumer drives a lot of the economy. If the consumer doesn't feel good, he likely won't spend money. If he doesn't spend money, then companies can't make money. And if companies don't make money, the markets likely won't recover. This line of thinking is not valid, primarily because the market isn't looking at today. The market is always looking at tomorrow. It cares little about where the economy is today and far more about where it is headed.

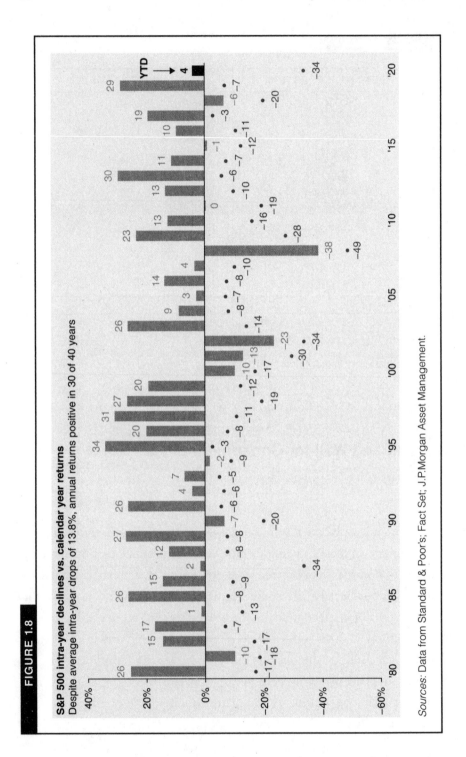

FIGURE 1.8

S&P 500 intra-year declines vs. calendar year returns
Despite average intra-year drops of 13.8%, annual returns positive in 30 of 40 years

Sources: Data from Standard & Poor's; Fact Set; J.P.Morgan Asset Management.

FIGURE 1.9

Consumer Confidence <60%	Next 12 Months (S&P 500)
1974	+37%
1980	+32%
1990	+30%
2008	+60%

Bull markets tend to emerge when investors are *feeling the worst* about the future outlook. The University of Michigan regularly measures consumer confidence. Figure 1.9 shows how the stock market performed the 12 months following each time consumer confidence was less than 60 percent.[22]

Learning to Accept the Bear Markets

If you are 55 years old, you can expect to live through about seven or so more bear markets. Do you really want to freak out every time? Are you really going to navigate through each one? No, you're not, because you know better! There is one great thing that all bear markets have in common: 100 percent of the time, they give way to bull markets. Not 50 percent of the time, not 75 percent of the time, not 99 percent of the time. 100 percent of the time! Why do so many people mess with those odds? It makes no sense. But alas, for most, investing isn't about common sense. It's about emotions and the perception of control. More on that later!

---

[22]My kids like to play the "opposite game," where you say the opposite of what you mean. Much of the market information that is intended to help investors, like the consumer confidence data, actually works the opposite of how commentators choose to reference it. We will see more of this later in the book when we look at Morningstar ratings.

Miscalculating the Risk of Market Timing

We have now established that market timing is dumb and doesn't work. You might be thinking, though, "What's the big deal? So what if I miss some gains in exchange for safety?" This is the main objection to investing rather than market timing. The answer is quite simple. The risk of being out of the market is far greater than being in the market.

Let's say you have $25,000, and you are deciding between investing and waiting for some arbitrary event to happen that will make you feel better about investing. If you invest all at once into a dividend-paying stock, one of three things will happen: The market will go up (hurray!), it will go sideways (very good—you get dividends!), or it will go down (still not a big deal because this is *temporary*). If it goes down, we know two things: First, we know you will collect dividends, which is better than what you get from cash, and second, we know the market will go back up. The downside is merely temporary—no big deal!

Now, if you wait in cash, the market can do the same three things: It can go up (you don't look so smart and lose a lot of money), it can go sideways (sorry, no dividends for you while you sit in cash), or it can go down (if you are too scared to go in today, are you going to feel better in the middle of a correction? Be honest with yourself. We both know the answer is "no"!). Now, here's the rub. If you are in cash and the market goes up, you may have permanently lost the opportunity to capture the upside. For example, the Dow moved quickly from around 20,000 to around 29,000. Yes, it may go back down, but will it go back to 20,000? Maybe, but maybe not. If it doesn't go back down to that level, the investor sitting in cash will never be able to capture that return again. Being on the sideline often results in *permanently* missing the upside. On the other hand, if someone invests today, the worst thing that can happen is *temporarily* participating in the downside. Big difference!

But What If I Am Perfect?

Oh, come on, really!? Well, there is always someone who thinks they can be perfect, that all the data and evidence don't apply to them, that they can find a way to make it happen. Let's look at just how much better

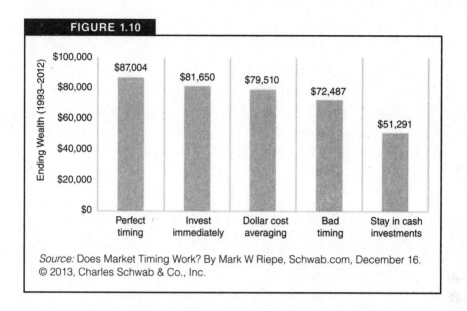

FIGURE 1.10

Source: Does Market Timing Work? By Mark W Riepe, Schwab.com, December 16. © 2013, Charles Schwab & Co., Inc.

off "that guy" will be if he is perfect. The Schwab Center for Financial Research evaluated five decisions available to an investor who has $2,000 in cash to invest once a year for 20 years (Riepe 2013):

1. Leave the money in cash.

2. Invest all at once each time.

3. Take the cash and dollar cost average into the market over the year, buying 1/12th each month.

4. Accidentally invest all of the money at the worst possible day every year (buying on the single day the market was the highest every single year).[23]

5. Fortuitously invest all of the money on the best possible day each year.[24] This is our Mr. Perfect. He always sits on the cash until the market is at the absolute lowest each year and then invests all the cash.

The results are nothing short of remarkable (see Figure 1.10).

---

[23]Wow, this person is unlucky! Or is he?

[24]I love this guy because he doesn't exist. He spends a lot of energy trying to convince you he is for real though.

The perfect market timer ended up with $87,004, and right behind him, in second place, is the person who invested the money as soon as they received it (Riepe, 2013).

Assuming you agree that you will not invest all the cash you get on the single best day you can every single year for 20 years, investing the cash right away seems like a pretty good idea. Everything else provides various degrees of losing. Losing isn't fun, especially when it is so easy to win.

Lump-Sum Investing versus Dollar-Cost Averaging

In the previous section, we covered why, if you find yourself getting money each year, you should invest it all at once instead of over time. But the advice is different if we are talking about a huge sum of money, right? Surely dollar-cost averaging instead of lump-sum investing spreads out the risk? After all, it's a common recommendation given repeatedly by financial pundits and advisors to invest a lump sum over time. Yet the answer is no, not really. It does, however, have legitimate psychological considerations that we will discuss in a minute.

First, what is a lump sum? A lump sum is when you get a boatload of money all at once. Examples are a large cash inheritance, proceeds from the sale of a business or real estate, a large gift (lucky you!), winning the lottery (super lucky you!), or a once-in-a-lifetime bonus. Lump-sum investing refers to taking this money and throwing it into the market all at once. Sounds crazy, right? Common wisdom says it's better to "dollar-cost average,"—that is, invest in the market over time, such as investing 1/12th of the lump sum each month for 12 months.

Vanguard conducted a study comparing lump-sum investing to dollar-cost averaging (Shtekhman, Tasopoulos, and Wimmer 2012). They used an example of an investor with a million dollars in cash to invest and ultimately wanted to be in a 60 percent stock and 40 percent bond portfolio. The researchers compared the impacts of lump-sum investing to dollar-cost averaging over 6, 12, 18, 24, 30, and 36 months. They also looked at the impact of this comparison in various markets, looking at the United States, the United Kingdom, and Australia. They then examined the impact of both strategies over 10-year rolling periods, going back to 1926. Finally, they repeated the study for various portfolios, ranging from 100 percent bond to 100 percent stock.

The conclusions are definitive. For an investor working their way to a 60/40 portfolio and holding it for ten years, *67 percent of the time, they ended up with more money by investing the lump sum instead of dollar-cost averaging over 12 months.* This result persists across the three countries (see Figure 1.11).

Furthermore, lump-sum investing's advantage was even more significant when compared to dollar-cost averaging over more extended periods (see Figure 1.12).

For example, in the U.S. market, lump-sum investing did better about 90 percent of the time compared to dollar-cost averaging over 36 months. At the end of the day, all the money is invested and invested most of the time. The only period that is different is the period an investor is dollar-cost averaging into the market.

So why does lump-sum investing perform better than dollar-cost averaging most of the time? The answer is simple: Bonds and stocks perform better than cash over time, and dollar-cost averaging leaves some of the investors' money in cash during the entry period.

Does that mean it is always best to lump-sum invest? Well, that depends on one crucial factor: you. Yes, the data is overwhelming that lump sum investing is better than dollar-cost averaging most of the time. However, just because something is statistically in your favor doesn't mean it is right for you. One thing to consider is the potential for regret.

We are all familiar with regret. We may regret something we said or something we didn't say, a risk we did or didn't take, the one that got away, or some other decision we did or did not make.[25] Psychologists have extensively studied the impact of regret on decision-making. This research has expanded into the behavioral psychology of investing.

---

[25]Right now, I am regretting eating a second helping of ice cream.

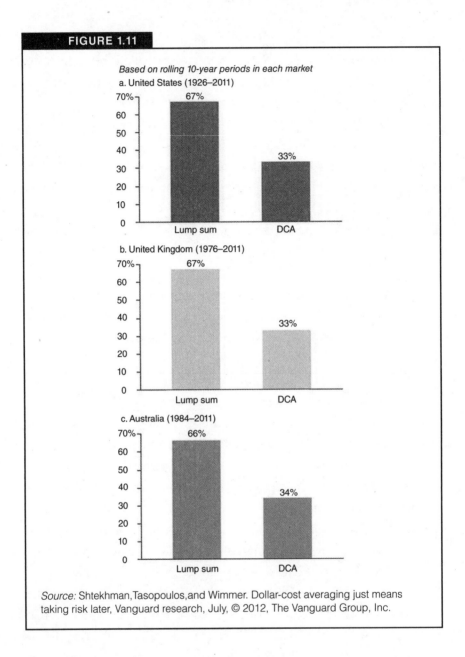

FIGURE 1.11

Based on rolling 10-year periods in each market
a. United States (1926–2011)

Source: Shtekhman, Tasopoulos, and Wimmer. Dollar-cost averaging just means taking risk later, Vanguard research, July, © 2012, The Vanguard Group, Inc.

One motivating factor for investors is fear of regret – the subconscious or fully conscious emotion that keeps us from selling a stock that is way up ("If I sell it, it may still go up and I'll regret it."), from selling a stock when it is down ("If I sell it, it may recover and I will regret it."), and

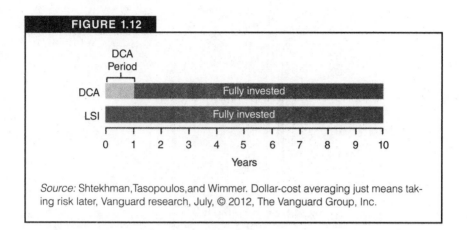

FIGURE 1.12

Source: Shtekhman, Tasopoulos, and Wimmer. Dollar-cost averaging just means taking risk later, Vanguard research, July, © 2012, The Vanguard Group, Inc.

from buying into the market when it is at an all-time high ("If I buy in, it may go down and I will regret it."). Fear of regret drives much of our decision-making and is a prevalent factor in investor behavior. Let's go back to you and assume you have had a lifetime event leaving you with a pile of cash to invest, and you are facing the lump sum investing versus the dollar-cost averaging decision. If you are the type of person who plays the statistics, doesn't get emotional about market movements, and won't experience debilitating regret if the market crashes the day after you invest, then lump-sum investing is for you. You will also likely be better off for it.

However, if you are the type of investor who will freak out if there is a market event (pick one—flash crash, tech bubble, 9/11, financial crisis, European debt crisis, etc.) the day after you invest, then spread it out a bit, and ease in over six months or so. Yes, you are most likely giving up some upside, but you will also be more likely to avoid regret and stick with the plan. In the end, the main point is to get invested—that's 90 percent of the game. The other 10 percent is getting invested as quickly as possible.

If you are going to dollar cost average, *commit to a calendar*, and invest as planned. For example, commit to investing 1/6th of the funds on the first Monday of every month until you are fully invested. Otherwise, you may fall into the paralysis trap of seeing how you feel about the market each month and sometimes hold back your investment. This is a loser's game. The stats say to lump-sum invest. The investor concerned with regret or willing to give up upside to avoid a short-term hit should consider dollar-cost averaging. Both should have a plan to invest and stick to it.

Learning to Fly

I'm learning to fly, but I ain't got wings

—Tom Petty

There comes a time when the baby birds need to leave the nest, take that jump, and learn to fly. Many investors have tried that before, only to land flat on their faces. Back in the nest, they struggle, looking for a time to "take the jump" again.

If we look back, there is no example in the stock market's history of taking a dollar from anyone. Someone who had no idea what they were doing and simply bought the S&P 500 would have made huge profits over the past 10, 20, or 30 years. However, truckloads of money have been lost by investors making mistakes with their portfolio or using advisors who have made market timing or security selection mistakes. It is hard for most to believe that had an investor bought into the market at any time in history, they would have more money today than if they stayed in cash.

Let's take a look at the unluckiest investors:

The one who invested right before the 1987 crash: S&P 500 at 334

The one who invested right before the early 1990s recession:
    S&P 500 at 363

The one who invested the day before 9/11: S&P 500 at 1,096

The one who invested the day of the 2007 stock market high:
    S&P 500 at 1,526

The one who invested the day before the coronavirus market panic: S&P 500 at 3,357. All of these unlucky individuals did much better than the bird that stayed in the nest, waiting for the "right time" to take the jump. *As of February 2021, the S&P 500 is at 3,773, but that does not*

*include dividends, which averaged over 2 percent along the way and is the equiva-
lent of approximately 516 more points since 2007.* Even the investors who
went in at the worst possible times are far ahead of the "investor" sitting
in cash, waiting for things to "settle down."

Many are scared off by the headlines that "the market is at an all-
time high." Well, that is often true, but it happens all the time. If that
sounds too scary to enter the market, the odds are high that you will
never be comfortable.

Of course, the reply to this argument is that it is always better to
enter after a market corrects or crashes. However, no one knows when
that will happen, or more importantly, how high the market will go
before it corrects. If the Dow goes from 25,000 to 26,000 then drops
back to 25,000, what have you accomplished in this scenario by sitting
in cash other than missing out on dividends? Also, I have yet to find the
investor who is nervous at Dow 25,000 but feels super-fantastic about
investing at Dow 23,000. If you are nervous when things are too good,
you will not feel better about investing when things don't look so hot.

For the disciplined investor, the time to invest is always today, and
that is only because yesterday is no longer an option. You are ready to fly
with the markets when you have the knowledge to serve as your wings.

Avoiding Mistake #1—Market Timing

The evidence is overwhelming that market timing does not work.
Academic research shows it, studies based on real-world managers
substantiate it, the masses get it wrong, the media gets it wrong, economists get it wrong, investment managers get it wrong, and so does just
about everybody else.

Market timing can be black and white, like going to cash and back to
stocks. Often you are market timing and don't realize it ("I'll hold onto
my bonus until the market settles."). Sometimes market timing is promoted by a money manager or financial advisor using coded language
like "asset-class rotation," "downside protection," "tactical asset allocation," "style rotation," or "sector rotation." It's all market timing. Part of
protecting yourself from this mistake is recognizing it.

Corrections are going to happen. Bear markets are going to happen. No matter how nervous you get or how bad things appear, the bear will give way to the bull. These corrections and bear markets will happen many times in your life, you can't predict them, and you will do more harm to your portfolio than good by trying to navigate your way through them by trading.

If an advisor tries to sell you any of these strategies, say "see ya later" and continue your search for another advisor. *If you are currently paying an advisor to do any of these things, know that you are willingly paying money to someone to increase your portfolio's odds of underperforming.* The research shows the pros can't do it. The odds are pretty darn high that you, your buddy, or your advisor can't do it either.

Active Trading

In 2019, there were 7,945 mutual funds in the United States and over 3,400 U.S. hedge funds, many of which trade U.S. stocks. On top of that, there are actively managed exchange-traded funds (ETFs) that do the same, and thousands of separately managed account managers, brokers, and investment advisors also trading U.S. stocks. For good measure, let's throw in tens of millions of regular, everyday people all over the world who also trade U.S. stocks. That's a lot of people trading. So how many U.S. stocks are all these people trading, you might ask?

Maybe 100,000 exchange-listed stocks? Nope. How about 25,000 exchange-listed stocks? Nope again. There are fewer than 4,400 companies listed on the public exchanges! Yep, that's right. Tens of thousands, if not hundreds of thousands, of professionals, plus tens of millions of other people are trading these 4,400 or so stocks.

It sounds silly—and it is. Pause for a moment and imagine a visual of tens of millions of people all in the same place trading a few thousand things back and forth. It's preposterous. Yet that's the active trading that takes place in the stock market every day.

If we combine the 4,400 or so exchange-listed stocks into one portfolio, they have a combined return called a *market return*. Common sense and basic arithmetic tell us that there must be winners and losers to the market return if people are trading within that portfolio. Here's the rub, though. Trading isn't free—there is always a cost. That means that there is a "house," you know, like Vegas. The house always wins. It gets paid no matter what. The house might be Merrill Lynch, UBS, Edward Jones, or one of the hundreds of other brokers out there, but there is always a house. So by definition, there must be more losers than winners, and the winners must win by enough to cover their transaction costs.

But wait, there's more. The winners must also pay taxes, a fact which moves many of the winners over to the losers' column. Sorry, guys!

What about the winners who win enough to cover transaction costs and taxes? Well, there is no evidence that winners stay winners. However, there is a tremendous amount of evidence, as we shall see, that winners from the past are generally not winners in the future and that eventually, most winners become big-time losers. There are various reasons for this, including that some winners were just lucky, or they took excess risk only to have that same excess risk backfire on them later, or they make one of many of the mistakes outlined in this book.

There is one thing that kills off almost all the winners: time. With time, winners in the stock trading game tend to become losers.

One study showed that over multiple 20-year periods, a portfolio with 500 of the largest stocks—held and never traded—would have out-performed over 80 percent of active traders (Ellis 2012). There are many reasons for this, and I will cover them now with the goal that you will, once and for all, be free of the temptation to play the trading game—a game the pros can't win and that you likely can't win either. It's a game for suckers. You are not a sucker.

The History of Active Trading

History doesn't repeat itself, but it rhymes.

—Mark Twain

From January 1, 1928, to July 1, 1932, Alfred Cowles researched traders' ability to beat the market (Cowles 1933). He reviewed 7,500 individual stock picks from 16 different financial services over a four-and-a-half-year period. He found that the professional stock-picking resulted in underperformance of 1.43 percent. In other words, only buying a bunch of stocks and doing nothing would have resulted in a much better outcome! Cowles went on to analyze the very best stock pickers' results and concluded that the outcome was attributable to luck more than skill (more on this topic later).

From 1928 to 1931, Cowles also studied 20 insurance companies' stock picks and found that they averaged an underperformance of 1.2 percent (Cowles 1933). Analyzing the winners, he found the best did not exhibit success due to skill, but rather by chance.

Nearly 100 years later, study after study shows that Cowles was onto something. Regardless of how sophisticated, expensive, or complicated, active management of stocks results in underperformance over long periods, *almost all the time.*

Active Investment Managers Lose to Indexing

Active trading is dead. That is not something you hear on CNBC of late.

Newsletters Lose to Indexing

Many investment newsletters offer market timing advice. As we discussed in Chapter 1, those letters don't do so well. The newsletters that provide stock picks don't perform so well either. Study after study shows that most newsletters don't even survive for ten years. As a group, those who survive lose to the market, and those who beat the market do not continue to beat the market (Graham and Campbell 1994). Particularly entertaining is a point Mark Hulbert made about going "all in" based on past performance. Looking at 1986 to 2006, Hulbert found that if you took $1,000,000 in 1985 and invested it per the recommendation of the previous year's top-rated newsletter, and repeated this strategy for all 16 years, you would have amassed $365, or an average annual loss of 31.4 percent (Young 2007)! Just because a newsletter is more right in its stock picks than all the others in any given year doesn't mean that you should put more money into their recommendations the next year!

Active Mutual Funds Lose to Indexing

On average, it's a simple fact that passive indexing always has and always will outperform active fund management—it's as certain as night follows day in this uncertain business.

—John Bogle

As we start, let's clear the air a bit. There is a raging debate in the investment world regarding whether passive management (owning a market index) beats active management (trading stocks in any given market). For example, a U.S. large-cap mutual fund manager's performance is often compared to the S&P 500 Index, a well-known U.S. large-cap index. Likewise, an international fund manager may be compared to the MSCI EAFE Index. There is an index (a large sampling of stocks) for every major market against which a manager's performance will be judged. The passive-versus-active debate is a heated one, but an illogical one. *It is a fact, not an opinion, that passive indexed investing, on the whole, handily beats active trading.* Let me repeat: This is a *fact*. Now, some would like to debate whether *some* active managers can beat the index. We will come to that later. For now, let's cover the evidence.

An actively managed fund's objective is to outperform its benchmark, whether it is the S&P 500 or any other index. Thanks to extensive databases tracking performance, many researchers have studied this topic. The S&P Dow Jones Indices publishes a report every year comparing actively managed funds to their respective benchmarks, and the results leave no room for doubt. In 2019, over 64% of large-cap fund managers underperformed the S&P 500, which was the ninth consecutive year that most funds had lagged the index. And it doesn't get any better the farther back you go; over ten years, 85.1% underperformed, and over 15 years, 91.6% underperformed! The performance gap isn't just limited to large-cap managers: over ten years, 85.7% of small-cap managers and 88% of mid-cap managers underperformed their respective benchmarks as well.

In the end, the conclusion of the report was definitive: "Over long-term horizons, 80% or more of active managers across all categories underperformed their respective benchmarks."

Survivor Bias (a.k.a. Mutual Fund Performance Is Even Worse Than the Data Suggests)

. . . if you look at the aggregate results of the mutual-fund industry on an after-fee, after-tax basis and adjust it for survivorship bias, the probability that you are going to end up with market-beating returns is de minimus . . . the 10-year after-tax shortfall for mutual funds is 4.5 percent per year relative to what you would have gotten if you had put your money in an index fund.

—David Swenson, Chief Investment Officer at Yale University, in an interview with the *Wall Street Journal's* Tom Lauricella in 2005

Mutual funds that underperform persistently are often closed. I don't mean closed to new investors; I mean, closed down, shut down, "dead." According to the S&P Dow Jones Indices fund manager report, from 2004 to 2019, 57% of domestic equity funds and 52% of all fixed-income funds were merged or liquidated. They found, unsurprisingly, that the main reason for the closure of the mutual funds was under-performance. Thus, fund managers' underperformance is *worse* than the data shows because it only accounts for the surviving funds' perfor-mance. It becomes even worse once the funds that closed are added back into the mix.

So what? Well, these funds are eliminated from databases that inves-tors use to make decisions. Survivor bias makes it appear as if these funds, often the worst performing of the bunch, didn't even exist at all! For example, Morningstar Principia, which tracks mutual fund perfor-mance, eliminates closed funds from its screens. In one comprehensive study, researchers added back all the closed funds from 1995 to 2004. They found that in 41 of 42 Morningstar fund categories, the result was a difference of −1.6 percent per year over the entire 10-year period (Barrett and Brodeski 2006). In other words, the actual performance of active mutual funds—which already as a group underperformed their index benchmarks—was actually 1.6 percent per year worse than the data suggests!

In another study, researchers examined 1,540 actively managed U.S. mutual funds from 1998 to 2012 (Wimmer, Chhabra, and Wallick 2013). They found that of those funds, only 55 percent survived, and the percentage that survived and outperformed was just 18 percent (see Figure 2.1).

The takeaway is straightforward: The data makes it clear that mutual funds underperform their respective benchmark indexes, and the data doesn't even accurately represent the degree of underperformance.[1]

What About the Winners, Huh? What About the Winners?!

Don't look for the needle in the haystack. Just buy the haystack!

—John Bogle

In any given year, there are winners. While the majority of mutual funds tend to lose to the index, some beat it. The issue is that they tend not to outperform consistently. We know that over time, performance almost always gives way to underperformance.

One great example of this is looking at the 50 hottest-selling mutual funds in 2000. They lost an average of 42 percent over the next five years, and only two of the funds made money over the five-year period. The

---

[1] It's dumbfounding that closed funds aren't included. Imagine that you were in a race against 10 people, and you came in first, but half the people were so out of shape that they couldn't finish the race. We would say you beat nine people, not four. When a team wins the World Series, we don't say they finished in first out of two teams; we include all the teams that didn't survive to make it to the World Series. The ones that didn't survive need to be included. Everyone seems to understand this concept except for money managers.

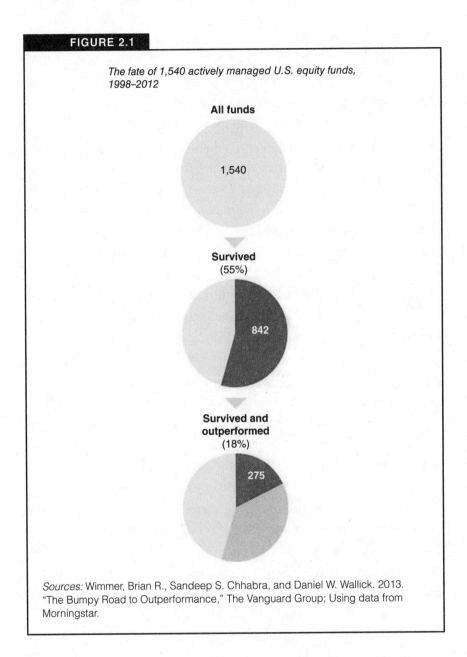

FIGURE 2.1

The fate of 1,540 actively managed U.S. equity funds, 1998–2012

All funds

1,540

Survived
(55%)

842

Survived and
outperformed
(18%)

275

Sources: Wimmer, Brian R., Sandeep S. Chhabra, and Daniel W. Wallick. 2013. "The Bumpy Road to Outperformance," The Vanguard Group; Using data from Morningstar.

losses were less severe for the 50 largest mutual funds: they "only" lost 15 percent over the same period. During that time, the S&P 500 Index was up just over 1 percent. Conversely, the 50 funds that saw the most redemptions in the 12 months ending March 2000 had gained an average of 21.4 percent[2] (Waggoner 2005). Investors pulled money from lower-performing funds and put the proceeds into the "hotter" funds. Unfortunately, the funds where people pulled the most money out later dramatically outperformed those "hotter" funds.

Let's take a more comprehensive look at the underlying phenomenon. Morningstar uses star ratings to evaluate mutual funds. If a fund scores in the top 10 percent of its category, it receives five stars; in the next 22.5 percent, four stars; in the middle 35 percent, three stars; in the next 22.5 percent, two stars; and in the bottom 10 percent, one star. Well, that makes it pretty easy. If a mutual fund has five stars, we should just buy it, right? Not so fast.

Analyzing data from June 1993 through December 2012, Vanguard plotted the mutual funds' performance for the 36 months after their star rating (The Vanguard Group, Inc. 2013b). (See Figure 2.2.)

The mutual funds that received five stars performed the worst, and those with one star performed the best. The star chart actually works in a reverse way than intended. Based on this study's findings, an investor is far more likely to outperform going forward by choosing a one-star-rated mutual fund!

If there are thousands of professional managers, surely some will outperform, if only because it is statistically normal for some to do so. Sometimes they outperform because they take excess risks, in which case those risks often come back to haunt them. The overall lesson, though, is that the short-term outperformance is usually due to luck or because a manager is taking excessive risks. The luck eventually runs out, or the risks eventually play out. There is a reason that investments have the disclaimer: "*Past performance is not an indicator of future results.*" That reason is that it is not indicative *at all* of future results!

---

[2] It's amazing how little patience investors have. They leave funds right before they recover and go into funds right before they collapse. Over and over and over again.

FIGURE 2.2

Source: Based on The Vanguard Group, Inc. 2013. "Vanguard's Principles for Investing Success."

The typical investor, unfortunately, doesn't understand any of this. And how could they when the entire industry, investment managers, and the media keep promoting the concept that recent outperformance means something? The consequences for the typical investor, though, are quite severe. Remember how the four- and five-star-rated funds have performed the worst going forward? *From 2000 to 2010, four- and five-star-rated funds took in 72 percent of all new assets placed into mutual funds* (Willoughby 2010). The pattern continues, and investors will likely continue to take shortcuts to evaluate investments that cause far more harm than good.

Hedge Funds Lose to Indexing

I want to pay more in fees, pay more in taxes, give up access to my investment, not know exactly what is going on with my money, and get below-average returns.
—Said no one, ever.

In 2008, Warren Buffett made a 10-year bet with Ted Seides, a partner at the hedge fund company, Protégé. Warren and Ted bet a million dollars, to be paid to the other's favorite charity, with Warren claiming that hedge funds could not beat the market, and Ted claiming that they most certainly can. Warren was so confident that he even let Ted choose the hedge funds rather than comparing the overall stock market's performance to the overall hedge fund market. In other words, this is a bet between owning the S&P 500, a fixed basket of stocks, and five hedge funds, the cream of the crop, hand-selected by Seides. Protégé's website claims that hedge funds beat the market while taking less risk.[3] Buffett claims that is all hooey and says hedge funds can't come close to justifying their fees.

I believe in using multiple asset classes, including stocks, bonds, real estate, commodities, and some publicly traded alternatives. However, there should be no place in a portfolio for equity hedge funds, which are hedge funds that invest in the stock market. There are lots of reasons, but the main one is simple: *Investing in hedge funds is a great way to increase the odds of* underperformance. This statement will likely contradict most of what you will hear about these investment vehicles, so let's look at the facts.

Hedge funds are private investment funds available to eligible investors who engage in a wide range of activities. Some hedge funds are "event driven," meaning they try to gain an edge on the markets based on significant events such as wars, oil shortages, economic events, and so on. Some are long/short funds, meaning they bet on some stocks going up and others going down. Some use derivatives and options, and many use leverage (borrow money to invest). Many of these funds' primary objective is to deliver the stock market return or an even better return with less volatility.

I never use equity hedge funds because I am well aware of what drives future performance, and hedge funds start with a disadvantage *in every category*: taxes, fees, risk management, transparency, and liquidity. First, for high-net-worth individuals, the top indicator of future performance, after asset allocation, is the tax effect of the investment. If the

---

[3] I hope you still have your BS meter on. These hedge fund guys take the cake by taking total garbage, making it look like candy, and selling the heck out of it.

investment is in a taxable account (not a tax-advantaged account, like an IRA or pension), the goal should always be to reduce taxes. Yet, hedge funds do the opposite: with active trading, nearly all hedge fund managers deliver a much larger tax hit than an index fund. Strike one.

Second, most hedge funds have ridiculously high fee schedules, with the typical fee being an annual management fee of 1.5 to 2 percent whether the portfolio is up or down, plus 20 percent of the profits (if there are profits).[4] Given that fees are a significant indicator of future performance, let's call this strike two.

Third, while we are on the subject of how hedge fund managers get paid, it is interesting to note that the manager has a great incentive to take huge risks with your money. If the manager gets paid 2 percent no matter what happens, plus a huge percentage of the profits, well, why not go for it? It is not uncommon for a hedge fund to go up 30 percent, make the manager a centimillionaire or billionaire, and then blow up a year later, with no negative consequence to the manager. This scenario occurred in 2012 when the top manager from the previous year saw his fund lose nearly half its value with abysmal performance. The consequence to the manager who made several billion the year before was simply a little embarrassment. He will likely get over it. I prefer to understand the risks in a given portfolio and control them. Strike three.

As if that isn't enough, hedge funds are not required to regularly disclose what they own or what their strategy even is at any given time. Therefore, the investor often has no idea what they own or the risks they are exposed to at any given period. They must wait for the statement to see what happened. I am a big believer in transparency. At any given time, you should know what you own and how your investments are doing and retain the flexibility to take appropriate action.[5]

---

[4] This is a big if. The failure rate of hedge funds is very high. More on that later.
[5] Hedge funds as an investment already struck out, so no need to keep counting strikes.

Finally, hedge funds lack liquidity. Hedge fund investors usually need to wait for "windows" to open to redeem their funds. Indexes provide liquidity, giving you the ability to exit positions at any given time. Now, why in the world would anyone invest in hedge funds when they know they will pay more taxes, pay fees 100 to 500 percent+ higher, take less control over their risk, lose transparency, and lose the ability to exit the investment whenever they wish? Well, the answer is quite simple: performance.

Only one problem: The hedge fund performance myth isn't a myth. It's a lie.

Credit Suisse has tracked the performance of hedge fund strategies through its AllHedge Index since 2004. How have the popular hedge fund strategies performed over time? Simply put: not well. The S&P 500 has outperformed hedge funds by an average of 7.5% *per year* since the inception of the study, and recent years have been particularly unkind, with the index outperforming hedge funds by 21.94% and 14.52% on average over a 1- and 3-year time frame.

Keep in mind, too, that most hedge funds perform so poorly, they don't even survive. According to Hedge Fund Research, more than 4,000 funds have closed since 2014, with more funds closed each year than new funds are being opened. In 2019, investors had pulled $81.5 billion out of hedge fund investments through November of that year, primarily because of poor performance. Jeff Vinik, the former Fidelity Magellan Fund manager, closed his funds and returned the money to his investors after earning a little over 4%. You may be thinking, "What about the best hedge funds?" The best hedge funds are the ones that often have the most spectacular downfalls. Long-Term Capital Management, run by Nobel Prize winners and considered the greatest hedge fund of its time, collapsed overnight and nearly took the markets down with it in 1998. Warren Buffett, who has repeatedly stated he finds hedge funds to be ridiculous investments, said of the Long-Term Capital Management fiasco: "They probably have as high an average IQ of any sixteen people working together in one business in the country . . . just an incredible amount of intellect in that group. Now you combine that with the fact that those sixteen had extensive experience in the field they were operating in . . . in aggregate, the sixteen probably had 350 to 400 years of experience doing exactly what they were doing. And then you throw in the third factor: that most of them had virtually all of their substantial net worths in the business . . . and essentially, they went broke . . . that to me is fascinating."

Bernie Madoff's hedge fund emerged as the new gold standard. A hard lesson regarding transparency was learned by many. Another hedge fund star, John Paulson, had predicted the 2008 mortgage crisis and used his hedge fund to bet correctly. His investors made huge returns, and he made billions, all in one year. Unfortunately for his investors, he lost 52 percent in 2011, when the market was up (Vardi 2012).

Hedge funds earned basically nothing during a full market cycle. From 2008 to the present, we saw an extended bull run where the S&P returned nearly ten times what the popular hedge fund strategies delivered over the same time frame. Where are the better returns with less risk? They simply don't exist. Instead, hedge funds have proven, once again, that they are handmade for suckers.

Hedge fund defenders[6] will say that while the purpose of hedge funds used to be to outperform the market, now the purpose is simply to reduce portfolio volatility. However, a study covering the period of 2002 through 2013 looked at the performance of hedge funds that primarily attempted to reduce volatility and compared the results to owning a simple 60 percent stock index, 40 percent bond index portfolio. The results showed that the simple indexed portfolio not only outperformed the hedge funds, *but it also did so with less volatility* (Housel 2014).

Now, back to the bet between Warren Buffett and Ted Seides. Let's just say it didn't go as planned for Ted. He threw in the towel with eight months to go. With the index up 85.4% to the hedge funds' cumulative return of 22%, it was the smart move.

Yes, hedge funds will make someone rich. Just likely not you.[7]

---

[6]Who are usually the people running or selling them.

[7]But the hedge fund managers will continue to laugh all the way to the bank or their yachts. How foolish they must think we all are. And we have given them plenty of reasons to think that.

Endowments—Misperception of Performance

We have all heard about endowments performing so well using alternative investments in their portfolio. How does that square with all the evidence that active investments like hedge funds don't work out so well?

To understand the difference, we need to understand the world of endowments.

Only around 14 percent of endowments manage $1 billion or more. We hear about these endowments all the time in the media—Yale, Harvard, and so on. A study examining publicity around endowments found that an investor was ten times more likely to hear or read a story about one of the ten largest endowments than one about the over 800 other endowments. These ten largest endowments, as a group, actually have at times done better than the market by a few percentage points over the last 25 years. However, it is essential to understand how they are doing it. They have vast teams of investors who are investing directly in many investments. For example, rather than buying into a hedge fund investing in timberland, the endowment directly buys the timberland. In fact, they do this 96 percent of the time (Wallick, Wimmer, and Schlanger 2012). Assuming you aren't going to buy a mine in Tanzania or 10,000 acres of land in Peru, this just isn't an option for you.

The other 86 percent of endowments haven't had much luck using hedge funds, private equity funds, active managers, and the like. These smaller endowments see the large endowments having success investing in alternative investments, so they buy them too. What they are missing is that the large endowments are having success because they buy *directly* and have a purchasing power advantage. Trying to replicate the success, smaller endowments, as a group, have increased their allocation to expensive alternative investments with small endowments now at 17 percent alternatives and medium endowments at 37 percent alternatives (Wallick, Wimmer, and Schlanger 2012). The results have not worked out well for them. Over the ten years ending June 30, 2011, the average endowment underperformed a simple 60 percent stock/40 percent bond index combination (Wallick, Wimmer, and Schlanger 2012). Even large endowments have struggled to sustain their performance; Harvard's endowment has underperformed the S&P 500 by several percentage points since 2007. The lesson here is unless you are a multibillionaire, forget about replicating the ten largest endowments. They are basically running a business by buying investments directly. Instead, outperform all the other endowments by avoiding indirect, expensive, underperforming investments like hedge funds.[8]

Venture Capital (Sounds Sexy but Usually a Dog)

We have met the enemy and he is us.

—Pogo[9]

Private equity investments are about as sexy as you can get, and the subset of venture capital—which is an investment in startups—is the coolest subset of the bunch. Many investors and even institutions have the misperception that venture capital funds produce outsized returns. Many of America's greatest companies were born from venture capital funds, including Google and Apple. The Kauffman Foundation, with its $2.3 billion fund, is one of the largest endowments in the country. In 2012, they released a groundbreaking paper on their experience with venture capital funds, aptly titled: "We Have Met the Enemy . . . and

---

[8]You might be thinking, "Come on. These endowments must be run by really smart people. Surely, they know all of this and wouldn't make these mistakes." Unfortunately, that's not the case. The financial services industry perpetuates misinformation and continually judges performance incorrectly. In fact, it is common industry practice for endowments to hire consultants who review the performance of hedge funds and mutual funds and then recommend the ones that performed the best over the last three or five years. This makes no sense and contributes to their perpetual underperformance.

[9]Pogo is not a philosopher or money manager. He is the main character of a comic strip from the 1940s that stayed popular through the early 1980s. For readers under 30, a comic strip is a sequence of drawings arranged into boxes to display humor, typically printed in a newspaper. (For those under 20, a newspaper is a printed publication of folded sheets containing news, articles, editorials, advertisements, and sometimes comic strips.)

He Is Us." I love the subtitle too: "Lessons from Twenty Years of the Kauffman Foundation's Investments in Venture Capital Funds and the Triumph of Hope over Experience."

The Kauffman Foundation analyzed their personal experience with 100 venture capital funds over 20 years. Among their findings were that the majority of venture capital funds underperformed the publicly available small-cap index; only 4 of 30 venture capital funds with over $400 million in committed capital outperformed the small-cap index, and the average venture capital fund ". . . fails to return the capital invested after fees." This finding is especially troubling since while the companies that venture capital funds invest in are small, they are much smaller than small-cap companies that comprise the publicly available index. Therefore, venture capital funds are far riskier. In other words, not only did venture capital funds underperform, they did so while taking more risk as well as charging higher fees (2 percent plus 20 percent of profits is the norm), less liquidity (investments often locked up for as much as a decade or more), and less transparency (what do we really know about what is going on in a private startup company anyway?).

The report's conclusion is straightforward: Investors are likely better off investing in a small-cap index fund than a venture capital fund. The researchers wrote, ". . . investors like us succumb time and again to narrative fallacies, a well-studied behavioral finance bias" (Mulcahy, Weeks, and Bradley 2012, p. 3). That is, investments in venture capital funds are based mainly on a story that looks backward to explain events and the allure of the promised higher returns.

Assuming you still have an interest in investing in venture capital and are confident the fund you invest in will do what the Kauffman Foundation's venture capital funds failed to do, note that unlike the Kauffman Foundation, a charity, you will owe taxes on any gains you receive. So if you can overcome the investment return odds, the tax gods will still set you back. For most investors interested in investing in an asset class with a high probability of outperforming large company stocks over ten years or more, small-cap index investing, not venture capital, is the answer.

The Taxman Cometh (a.k.a. Dear Goodness, It Gets Worse)

Should five percent appear too small, be thankful I don't take it all, 'cause I'm the taxman, yeah I'm the taxman.

—"Taxman" from the Beatles Album, *Revolver*

When a mutual fund, hedge fund, or index fund publishes its returns, it is always showing you *pre-tax* returns. Keep in mind that the entire point of an actively managed fund is to outperform a specific benchmark or index; otherwise, there is no point in using the manager. Well, to beat the index, the active manager usually trades securities. The fund doesn't pay the taxes that result from the trading; you do! The average mutual fund loses a full percent, *every year*, to taxes (The Vanguard Group, Inc. 2013a). So, if the mutual fund performance shows a return of 6 percent, it's actually 5 percent after you pay the taxman. The results are even worse for hedge fund managers who are, as a group, even more active traders. Index funds have tax consequences too, as stocks are added to or dropped off the index, but because there are no active traders, the consequences are far less.

At the end of the day, it doesn't matter what you earn. What matters is what you earn *after taxes*. Keep in mind that indexes beat active managers even before taxes are taken into consideration. Taxes just widen the performance gap even further.

Portfolio Activity Hurts Performance

My favorite holding period is forever.

—Warren Buffett

We know that mutual funds, hedge funds, and investment managers who trade stocks underperform the index as a group. Research not only shows that active trading underperforms but that the more active the manager is, the more likely they are to underperform.

Brigham Young University professor Craig Israelsen examined U.S. stock, U.S. bond, and International Stock mutual fund managers' returns over 3-, 5-, and 10-year periods (Israelsen 2010). He divided the funds into four groups based on how actively they trade.

In every single case, and over every period, the funds with the most activity underperformed the funds with the least activity. *In other words, the more active and involved the manager, the worse the funds performed!* Over ten years, the low turnover U.S. managers outperformed the high turnover managers by 2.2 percent *per year*, with the outperformance of low turnover International managers at 1.6 percent per year and low turnover bond managers at .2 percent per year.

The less the manager traded, the better the investors did. If you want to trade way less, skip the mutual funds, skip the hedge funds, skip the investment managers who actively trade, and focus the core of your portfolio on indexes.

But Doesn't Active Management Work in a Down Market?

Bear markets happen all the time. When they happen, managers flood TV, radio, and letters saying that active management is needed more than ever, keeping a popular myth alive: the myth that active managers can at least outperform when the market is down. It is just a myth, though: In the seven bear markets since 1973, active managers outperformed just three times (Philips, Kinniry, and Schlanger 2013). They didn't make up for it when things turned around either, underperforming in six of the last eight bull markets (Philips, Kinniry, and Schlanger 2013). Overall, active managers lose in up markets, sideways markets, and down markets; they just underperform by a smaller percentage in a down market.

When we look at modern-day bear markets, from 2000 to 2002, the 2008 crisis, and the coronavirus pandemic, the results are the same. In every major category, the index beat the active manager (see Figure 2.3). During the 2020 market crisis, 74% of active managers underperformed

FIGURE 2.3

Percent of Active Funds Outperformed by Benchmarks in Bear Markets		
Fund Category	2008	2000 to 2002
All Large-Cap Funds	54.3	53.5
All Mid-Cap Funds	74.7	77.3
All Small-Cap Funds	83.8	71.6

the S&P 500 between February 19 and April 30. In short, active managers delivered the worst returns at the exact moment they were supposed to provide the most value.

Why Indexes Win

Passive investing beats active investing for several reasons. First, active trading dilutes returns due to transaction costs; second, active management costs substantially more; third, active management generates more taxes; fourth, the typical active manager sits on more cash than an index fund, and this cash drag hurts returns over time; and fifth, active managers fall prey to the same behavioral mistakes that everyday investors make (more on this later).

There is another big reason why indexes outperform: the variance of returns among stocks. Most people think an index contains a basket of stocks, half of which outperform the market and half of which underperform the market. The fact is that within an index, nearly two-thirds of stocks underperform the index itself, while about one-third outperform. How can this be? It's because when a stock goes down, the worst thing that can happen is a loss of 100 percent (see Lehman Brothers, Enron, MF Global, and so on). However, when a stock takes off, the sky is the limit—the return can go up thousands of percentage points (see Apple, Google, Microsoft, and so on). A big winner can offset many losers. If you have a basketball team with ten players and the team scores 100 points, we don't assume half scored more than ten and half scored less than 10. In reality, one or two players can score the majority of the points. It's the same with the market. By casting a wide net with the index, you are more likely to catch the next high flyer.

But Indexing Results in Average Returns

Indexing does not result in average returns—it all but guarantees that over time, you will have above-average returns. The only question is how much above-average the returns will be. Most of the time, the returns are far above average. Over the 20 years ending January 1, 2014, indexes in various categories outperformed 71 to 85 percent of actively managed funds (The Vanguard Group, Inc., 2013b). Does that sound average to you? Indexing will put you in the winner's circle if you let it.[10]

S&P 500, Here I Come!

Don't put all your eggs in one basket.

—English proverb

Well, then. Let's toss all our money in the S&P 500 and move on with life! Not so fast. Investing doesn't need to be overly complicated, but it's not that easy. Let's look at a recent decade to see why asset allocation matters.

Much has been made about the negative return of the market from 2000 through 2010.

It is enlightening to put one of the worst decades in stock market history into proper context. First, commentators often refer to this decade as the "Lost Decade," and cite it as proof that owning the market doesn't work. Actually, it is a testament to quite the opposite conclusion.

---

[10]And you need to let it!

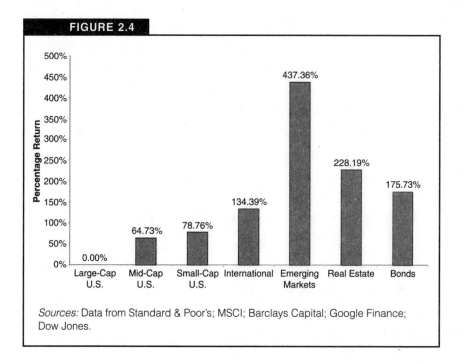

FIGURE 2.4

Sources: Data from Standard & Poor's; MSCI; Barclays Capital; Google Finance; Dow Jones.

First, it is important to note that when people say "the market" lost money over that decade, they are referring to the S&P 500 Index. In fact, this index represents just part of the market: The S&P 500 is comprised of exclusively large-company, U.S. stocks.

A graph tells the story quite nicely (see Figure 2.4).

As with all previous bear markets, the well-allocated investor weathered the storm quite nicely. By properly allocating the portfolio, the investor not only took on less risk, but also earned better returns. Since it is impossible to identify which asset class will outperform on a year-by-year basis, the prudent investor invests for the long run and *is never dependent on the short-term performance of one market.*

The next time someone talks to you about the "Lost Decade" as a reason to market-time or actively trade stocks, remind them that a simple asset allocation made the decade quite profitable for a sensible investor. The other markets—real estate, emerging markets, international, and mid-cap and small-cap U.S. markets—were up.

Also, charts like the one used here actually understate how well the investor actually performed. The S&P 500, in fact, was actually up a few percentage points when dividends are included, and since the investor received them, it seems sensible to count them. All in all, while owning just the S&P 500 would have been extremely unpleasant, someone who simply allocated their portfolio across various asset classes and ignored the assault of bear markets throughout the decade did quite well, even during one of the worst periods in all history to be an investor.

Avoiding Mistake #2—Active Trading

We know that simple math tells us the majority of active managers—whether mutual fund managers, hedge fund managers, brokers, investment managers, or you—must underperform. We also know that active management costs more than owning an index. Let's add on that active managers create more taxes than passive managers. Finally, we know when we do find an active manager who outperforms, there is no evidence that suggests the outperformance will continue. In fact, there is extensive evidence suggesting quite the opposite.

So, we know with certainty we will pay more in fees. We know with certainty we will pay more in taxes. We know there is a high probability of underperformance even before fees and taxes. This seems pretty clear. Maybe active management isn't the way to go.

With all of this knowledge, why do so many of us actively trade, hire fund managers who trade, or hire investment managers who trade? Because we all want to believe it can be done. We are Americans, for goodness sakes! Someone can always outperform, there is always a way to beat the street or to game the system. Well, if you hand your money to an active manager, someone is getting gamed alright. It's you.

Misunderstanding Performance and Financial Information

Many myths persist in the investment management field; a few because of investors' biases, some because they make for cute stories in the media, and many because professionals encourage and perpetuate them. In this chapter, we will take a look at some of the most common misperceptions.

Misunderstanding #1—Judging Performance in a Vacuum

A friend shared with me the performance of a money manager they were considering. The manager was essentially saying, "Hey, look at how awesomely this portfolio has performed; put your money in this!" While this may literally be the single worst way to decide on investments, this is how most Americans choose their portfolio.

So what's the problem? The problem is a function of misunderstanding "reference sets." Reference sets can best be explained this way: Assume you have a room full of 12,000 people and tell them to each flip a coin. If you repeat this about 13 times, someone will likely have flipped heads every time. We should not marvel at the brilliance of such a person. Instead, we should expect this outcome.

Similarly, if we visit a Las Vegas casino and find someone winning at roulette, we don't hand them all of our money. We know this is one gambler in a reference set full of gamblers and that most of them are losing. In his book, *The Black Swan*, Nassim Taleb calls this "the reference point argument," which he describes as not computing odds from the vantage point of a winning gambler, but from that of all the gamblers who started at the same time (Taleb 2007). We know that some people give their money to the "hot hand" gambler to bet for them. These people are shortsighted and exhibit the same behavior as an investor giving their money to the latest fund manager on a winning streak.

It is also how most money managers market their success stories. For example, it is not uncommon for a money manager to manage 6 to 10 portfolios or funds. Not surprisingly, one or two of these are likely to outperform their benchmark. Slick glossies and PowerPoint presentations are then made to tout the performance, completely ignoring the majority of portfolios or funds that did not meet or beat their benchmark. Then investors buy in; the fund eventually underperforms, so the manager then touts another portfolio, and the investor moves to the next hot hand . . . and so on.

Mutual fund companies use the same strategy. As with all decades, from 2000 to 2010, most large company mutual fund managers underperformed the S&P 500. That is quite a spectacular feat considering the S&P 500 itself was barely positive over the decade (assuming dividends are included). You would never know it when looking at the advertisements from mutual fund companies, though!

Whenever a money manager who is trading stocks in one market tries to sell you on their performance, ask them for the performance of all of their strategies. The full reference set will expose the outperformance of one or two strategies as what they really are: one of many expected outcomes. Of the vast reference set of mutual funds and hedge funds, the overwhelming majority underperform, *and there is no evidence the winners will continue to win.*

This is why you should always ignore a particular investment manager's past performance and question what type of money manager would choose to market himself that way in the first place. Suppose you are working with an advisor who considers your personal situation—taxes, state of residence, outside holdings, etc. In that case, the portfolio should be customized to the point that they cannot show past model performance anyway.

A trader's past performance in any given market has little or no bearing on their expected future performance. Under most circumstances, the key to understanding why a manager has outperformed over a period of time is to look at the entire field. For example, the few professional traders who were able to beat the S&P 500 over a given 10-year period should not be viewed as the active managers to hire going forward. Instead, they should be seen as a great example of a field full of carnage, one that an intelligent investor should avoid altogether.

Misunderstanding #2—Believing the Financial Media Exists to Help You Make Smart Decisions (a.k.a. the Media Is Killing You)[1]

Do you know what investing for the long run but listening to market news every day is like? It's like a man walking up a big hill with a yo-yo and keeping his eyes fixed on the yo-yo instead of the hill.

—Alan Abelson

---

[1]A special note to all you English majors: Yes, we are aware that "media" is plural and therefore using "the" before media is not necessary, and even considered incorrect. We researched this a bit and have found "media" widely accepted in the singular for several decades. We also think it just sounds better than saying "media is killing you." Since we have space, here is our defense:

> The etymologically plural form media is often used as a singular to refer to a particular means of communication, as in, *the Internet is the most exciting new media since television*. Many people regard this usage as incorrect, preferring medium in such contexts. People also use media with the definite article as a collective term to refer not to the forms of communication themselves so much as the communities and institutions behind them. In this sense, the media means something like "the press." Like other collective nouns, it may take a singular or plural verb depending on the intended meaning. If the point is to emphasize the multifaceted nature of the press, a plural verb may be more appropriate: The media have covered the trial in a variety of formats. Frequently, however, media stands as a singular noun for the aggregate of journalists and broadcasters: The media has not shown much interest in covering the trial. This development of a singular media parallels that of more established words such as data and agenda, which are also Latin plurals that have acquired a singular meaning. (*The American Heritage Dictionary of the English Language*, 4th edition, 2000)

It seems that no matter which direction the market is heading, there is always a chorus of vocal fatalists that dominate the financial media.

Of course, this is nothing new. Financial media have been selling fear dating back to the 1907 crash. Many books have been written citing how incorrect the financial media have been about its more recent predictions, such as the 1970s stagflation, the 1987 crash, the tech bubble (which took hysteria to an entirely new level since it accompanied the rise of 24-hour televised financial news), 9/11, the 2008 crisis, and the European debt crisis.

Yet every bear market has given way to a bull market, and every economic contraction has given way to economic expansion. One would think that the financial media would be reassuring during a time of crisis, especially since there is one about every three to five years. So, why is that not the case?

During any crisis (debt ceiling crisis, fiscal cliff, European debt, whatever), many pundits will encourage viewers to go to cash, and many money managers will do just that, all with the purpose of "protecting" assets. Those who follow their advice often permanently miss the gains that occur as the crisis subsides.

The main issue with financial media is that many who consume it fail to understand the purpose of its existence. Media is business, and businesses exist to make a profit. The primary purpose of CNBC, FOX Business News, CNN, and your local radio station is not to inform; it is to make money. They exist, quite simply, to make a profit.

The profit is made by selling advertisements. The ads are sold at higher prices on shows and stations with higher ratings. Therefore, the primary purpose of any financial show is to get as many viewers as possible (they call them "eyeballs") and to get those viewers to watch for as long as possible.

The rough math is:

More viewers = higher prices for commercial space
= larger profit = happier shareholders

To get viewers, shows often overdramatize and draw out events. Many events are packaged into stories with a tag line, storyline, and story arch. Often, it is accompanied by what screenwriters call "putting a clock on it."[2] Just as a movie will create tension and a sense of urgency with a ticking clock ("If Sandra Bullock doesn't get to the space station in 90 minutes, she will get hit by space junk and die!"),[3] the financial media matches many of these stories with a clock in the lower right-hand corner of the screen. Tick, tick, tick. Just think of the "The Sequester," "The Fiscal Cliff," and so on. For a recent example, recall the clock winding down, by the minute (really, we need by the minute?) to the Debt Ceiling limit. To further tie viewers to the set, producers and hosts will often press guests for short-term market calls. These tactics often cause viewers to panic and make mistakes.

How many retirement plans were messed up when some viewers went to cash during the fiscal crisis, the government shutdown, the debt ceiling talks, or the coronavirus-fueled market meltdown? In their study titled "Financial News and Client Stress," Dr. John Grable of Kansas State University and Dr. Sonya Britt of the University of Georgia found that *an individual's stress level increases substantially while viewing financial news, regardless of what the financial news is about* (Grable and Britt 2012). When the market is going down, people are worried about their accounts, and when the market is going up, people are upset they are not more aggressively positioned!

The study found that 67 percent of people watching financial news on CNBC, Bloomberg, Fox Business, and CNN showed increased stress levels. *Even when the financial news was positive, 75 percent exhibited signs of increased stress* (Grable and Britt 2012).

---

[2]Thanks to my brother, Mark, a screenwriter for sharing this concept with me. For free.

[3]This is a reference to the 2013 blockbuster *Gravity*, and not to be confused with the "If Sandra Bullock doesn't help disarm a bomb on this bus before it drops below a certain speed, everyone will die!" which would be a reference to the 1994 blockbuster *Speed*.

Physicians often tell their patients to control their stress levels because stress and anxiety greatly increase the probability of sickness, disease, and even death.[4]

Not to mention that it is simply not fun to be stressed out. From a financial perspective, there is another side effect of stress that can cause immediate damage: People tend to make poorer decisions when under stress. The classic example is the investor who watches a lot of financial news and reacts in a panic, creating permanent losses in their portfolio.

In my experience, I have noticed that those who are too busy to watch the financial media closely rarely make mistakes. On the other hand, it is not uncommon for a retiree who watches a lot of financial news to make a significant trading decision with negative consequences.

No one is saying the media creates a crisis.[5] I am merely saying the media is not motivated to educate and reassure the viewer because that would reduce viewership. It is likely not a coincidence that one of the most interviewed economists on CNBC is the persistently ominous Nouriel Roubini. You may recall his nickname, Dr. Doom.

It is not unlike The Weather Channel, which has its regular viewers. However, nothing stirs up viewership like a hurricane or tornado. The meteorologist can hardly contain his glee, knowing ratings are very high. Unlike a hurricane, which leaves even the prepared with permanent damage on occasion, every bear market storm has passed, leaving the well-positioned and reasoned investor 100 percent intact.

This is not to say all media is bad (it is not), that all news is full of hyperbole (some is not), or that everyone who watches financial news, even lots of it, gets stressed out (just most of them). *It does mean, though, that if you are watching a lot of financial news, you should take a moment to ask yourself what you are getting out of it and how it makes you feel.*

---

[4]If you are asking, "Did Peter basically just allege that the news can kill you?" Well, if you watch too much of it and get worked up about it, then yes, I did!
[5]Actually, some people do say that, or that the media at least contribute to some crises.

More importantly, if the stress gets to you, do not let it impact your decision-making or keep you from following your strategy. The key to having a successful, repeatable investment strategy is to stay disciplined, and a core component of staying disciplined is to recognize and shut out the noise.

Misunderstanding #3—Believing That the Market Cares About Today

Although it's easy to forget sometimes, a share is not a lottery ticket . . . it's part ownership of a business.

—Peter Lynch

If a business does well, the stock eventually follows.

—Warren Buffett

People often ask the question: What makes the stock market move up or down? Some are confident that they know the answer, but they are almost always wrong.

People will often cite one of the following as being the primary driver of stock prices: unemployment, housing, economic policy, monetary policy, the strength of the dollar, consumer confidence, retail sales, and interest rates. All are popular choices. In order, the answer to each of these is no, no, no, still no, no, no again, no, and another final no.

The stock market cares about only one thing above all else: *anticipated earnings.* If companies make more money, their share prices eventually rise. The stock price is simply a reflection of a company's earning power. *Everything else is noise.*

Assume for a moment that you are going to buy a sandwich shop. What do you care about? The only factor you care about is anticipated earnings. If you buy the sandwich shop, you are doing so because you believe the profits earned will justify the purchase price with a good return.

To arrive at this conclusion, though, you will look at other factors that will affect your ability to make money owning this sandwich shop.

For example, if interest rates are low, you will make lower payments on your loan, thus making the shop more profitable. In this case, interest rates only matter because they affect your anticipated earnings. Commodity prices will also likely matter, as oil and food are commodities. If oil prices go up, it will cost more to have the food delivered to your shop every day. Rising food costs increase your expenses as well. Both increases in commodity prices eat away at your bottom line, thus hurting anticipated earnings. Consumer confidence matters because if consumers think their financial world is collapsing, they will forgo your $8 sandwich and make the kids a PB&J at home. That will drive down sales, which would impact your earnings. You get the idea.

Note, however, the critical word here is "anticipated." No one cares about yesterday's earnings. For example, let's go back to that sandwich shop you want to buy. You are talking to the owner, reviewing his financials, and you can see he made $100,000 each of the last three years, selling about 20,000 sandwiches a year. It sounds pretty stable, so you are thinking about offering him $200,000 for his business, knowing that you can make $100,000 per year once you pay off the debt it takes to buy it. But you are too smart for that. You notice that he sells 5,000 of his sandwiches each year to a large corporate client. That client just went out of business. If you back those sales out, the sandwich shop would be much less profitable, so you would no longer offer the same price. You are focused on the only thing that matters: *anticipated earnings*.

The bottom line is this: All of the other factors in the economy matter only because people buying and selling stocks are trying to determine how the changes in various "indicators"—like unemployment, interest rates, etc.—will ultimately affect a company's anticipated earnings. No one cares how much health care companies made in the past.

They want to know how the new healthcare reform laws will impact these companies' future earnings. No one cares if Starbucks made a million or a billion last year. They want to know if their earnings will be hurt now that McDonald's is selling gourmet coffee. No one cares how much money General Dynamics made selling military supplies to the government in the past. They want to know if military conflicts will persist, driving up future sales.

That is why when the U.S. bear market was in full swing, investors bought Walmart stock. The thought was that Walmart's earnings would likely go up as consumers moved "downstream" to buy everything as inexpensively as possible. The same reasoning drove Nordstrom's stock price down. McDonald's did fine as investors figured consumers would want to eat out on the cheap. The same logic drove down the stock price of higher-end restaurants like the Cheesecake Factory. Of course, companies selling alcohol did fine as people tend to drink when they are depressed (and when they are happy, which is why alcohol is considered "recession proof").

The stock market as a whole tends to move up well before a recession is over. It does not care what is going on today. It is anticipating the earnings of companies in the future. If the stock market drops, it is because investors believe future earnings will get worse. If the market moves up, it is because investors believe the economic climate is changing to enable companies to become more profitable in the future.

Of course, so many variables go into guessing anticipated earnings that the market is not always right in the very short term (even though it is always right in the long run). For example, you can buy the perfect sandwich store in perfect condition and then have a multitude of surprises derail your profits, like a crime in the area, unforeseen road construction blocking access to your shop, and so on. Likewise, we can have a nearly perfect economic environment, and someone can fly a plane into a building and turn everything upside down overnight.

However, unlike your sandwich store, which can go to zero, the stock market itself is resilient. Every time in history, no matter how bad things have appeared, U.S. companies as a whole have ultimately found a way to not only make money, but to make more money than they did before. Every single time. And, as always, the stock market will continue to follow the earnings.

Misunderstanding #4—Believing an All-Time High Means the Market is Due for a Pullback

Stock Market Hits All-Time High. Now What?

—CNBC.com, April 10, 2013[6]

I think the market is a little frothy, and I have cashed out all my positions.

—Steve Grasso, Director of Institutional Trading
at Stuart Frankel, in the same article

Don't get scared because of an "all-time high."

Whenever the market breaks through to a new high, there is talk of a bubble. Every time any market moves into new territory, the talk of a correction or bear market gets more and more incessant. You can count on it. Watching and reading the coverage regarding the Dow passing any landmark can make one's head spin.

One point of view is that once the Dow passes a "barrier," the average investor will jump back into the market, and professional traders who have been sitting the market out will have to get back in, both driving the stock market much higher.

The more common slant is that the Dow, having plowed through a new threshold, is ripe for a pullback. The market, they argue, has come too far, too fast. Both crowds don't understand that Dow 18,000, 20,000, 25,000, and 30,000 are just numbers, and for the most part, mean nothing. The latter crowd is also primarily comprised of the "investors" who sat in cash while contemplating the pullback that would accompany the previous Dow threshold breakthrough.

First, simply because a market is at a new high does not automatically qualify it as a "bubble." A bubble is when an asset class trades at a level far beyond its intrinsic value. In the not so distant past, we have watched

---

[6]The stock market has hit well over 250 all-time highs since then. All of these "events" have been accompanied by commentators talking about things like "being overdue for a correction," the market being "frothy," how it's time for a "pullback," and the like.

a few bubbles burst. One was the tech bubble, when technology stocks were trading approximately five times higher than their historical valuation level. Another was real estate, which was trading at more than 50 percent above its historical valuation level when it finally burst.

So, to determine if the U.S. stock market is a bubble, we need to understand how stocks are valued in the first place. As with all asset classes, there are many ways to value stocks. However, the most referenced calculation is the P/E ratio. The P/E ratio is calculated by taking the stock price and dividing it by the company's earnings. For example, if a stock is at $100 per share, and the earnings are $5 per share, then the P/E ratio is 20. Stock prices can go up and the market can keep hitting new highs but remain fairly valued.

To illustrate this concept, let's step into the real estate market for a moment. Let's say that the typical residential real estate investment yields an investor 10 percent. An investor searches the market and finds a duplex to buy for $100,000. The investor rents out the duplex, and after paying the cost of taxes, maintenance, and insurance, makes an annual profit of $10,000. The investor is making 10 percent and is quite happy.

A few years go by, and the economy has recovered a bit. Renters can afford to pay more, so the investor charges more rent, and his annual profit is now $15,000.

A new investor comes along and wants to buy a property to earn the typical residential real estate return of 10 percent. The new investor pays the previous owner $150,000 for his duplex as the profits are now $15,000, which will net him 10 percent.

The value of the duplex went from $100,000 to $150,000 because the earnings went up. Although the price is up 50 percent, the expected return is still the same. However, if the duplex had gone up in value from $100,000 to $150,000, with the profit staying at $10,000, we would have a "bubble," meaning the investment price is much higher than the historical average. Bubbles tend to end badly. They always eventually burst. A bubble is not defined by rising prices alone; rather, a bubble is defined by rising prices relative to earnings.

The stock market does not sort of work like this; it works exactly like this.

The stock market exemplified this concept during its ride from the S&P 500 at 1,100 to the S&P 500 at 3,200. When the S&P was at 1,100, the market was trading at 20.7 times earnings. When it was at 3,200, the market was trading at 19.6 times earnings. In other words, by this measure, the market was a better value at 3,200 than it was at 1,100. Even though the market's annualized growth during this time frame was over 12.5%, it was outpaced by the growth of corporate earnings over the same period.

It is also important to remember that it does not matter how high a stock price goes; instead, it is how high it goes relative to its earnings. A company making $10 million per year with a share price of $100 may one day go on to make $15 million per year, at which point no one should be surprised if the stock trades at $150.

Finally, of note is that the market hits all-time highs all the time, more often than once a month on average. Basic inflation is responsible for a portion of the gains. As I type this, I am drinking a Diet Coke, currently selling at an all-time high. I wish I could eat a candy bar as well. They are also selling at all-time highs. If you purchased this book[7] through the mail, it would have been mailed with stamps that are also priced at an all-time high. Almost everything is at an all-time high most of the time, whether it is a meal at McDonald's, a car, or the cost to build a house. When you buy your turkey for the holidays, it will likely not be selling at an all-time low. The same goes for your new car, a new shirt, or new jewelry.

The Dow flirting with thresholds is psychological; ultimately, it means nothing. Market prices, like all investments, follow earnings. And for the long-term investor, that is all that matters. The next time you read that the market has hit an "all-time high," shrug and smile. It's no reason to panic.

---

[7] Thank you!

Misunderstanding #5—Believing Correlation Equals Causation

A black cat crossing your path sometimes signifies an animal is going somewhere.
—Groucho Marx

Just because something happens often, or appears to maintain a pattern, does not mean that there is an actual cause and effect taking place. Scientists, doctors, and statisticians learn in introductory classes that "correlation does not mean causation."

For example, there is a predictive measure known as the "Super Bowl Indicator." The stock market tends to do well when the NFC wins and mediocre when the AFC wins. This indicator has been about 80 percent accurate. Nevertheless, its value going forward as an indicator is 0 percent. There is also a predictive measure known as the "*Sports Illustrated* Swimsuit Edition Indicator." When the cover model is American, U.S. stocks tend to perform better than their historical average. When the cover model is not American, U.S. stocks tend to perform worse than their historical average. While this has resulted in quite remarkable results with a more than 6 percent per year difference in returns, this indicator's value is, of course, worthless as well.

While we can have fun with this sort of stuff, no one takes it seriously. Or do they? Let's look at a few popular recurring stories.

October Is The Worst Month to Invest

October: This is one of the peculiarly dangerous months to speculate in stocks. The others are July, January, September, April, November, May, March, June, December, August, and February.

—Mark Twain

In late September, I met with a prospective client who wanted to wait to invest his account until November because of articles he had read about how poorly stocks perform in October.

Almost every month, the financial media release stories about the historical trends of a particular month. A 2012 CNN article went over all the terrible things that have happened in the market during October (Voigt 2011).

These articles reiterate a perception that there are "good times" and "bad times" to be invested and that some easy rules of thumb—such as not investing in the market in October—can be followed to achieve better returns.

Unfortunately, it is just not that easy. These articles are classic examples of the media giving investors data that makes them less knowledgeable about investing than before reading the information.

Even if the October pattern were relevant, it sure does not hold much water. Articles on why not to invest in October state that the pattern looks quite reliable if you leave out specific periods. It is like saying that the Denver Broncos have the best Super Bowl winning percentage if you exclude their five title game losses, or that Republicans have won every modern presidential election if you leave out the Obama, Clinton, Carter, and Biden administrations. You cannot just leave out entire pieces of a data set as if they are irrelevant exceptions!

Sell in May and Go Away

Market timing does not work, at least not using Sell in May and Go Away. As with most market-timing strategies, a little bit of analysis often reveals the devil in the details.

—Rick Ferri, *Forbes* (2013)

The "Sell in May and Go Away" theory holds that investors should sell their stocks at the beginning of May and re-enter the market at the beginning of November. This theory is promoted on the idea that the market has historically performed better during the November through April six-month period than the May through October six-month period. It is true that historically the stock market, at first glance, has had a better return during the November through April time period. But does this correlation imply causation? Many people believe it is real and persistent, arguing that traders take the summer months off. Another theory posits that investors receive much of their money at year-end or the beginning of the year and invest it. For our purposes, let's assume that yes, we believe that this anomaly will persist.

A recent study by CXO Advisory Group looked back at a 142-year period of the market ending in 2012 (CXO 2013). The return of a simple buy-and-hold strategy dramatically outperformed the "Sell in May" strategy. The gap is much higher when portfolio friction, the impact of costs, are included. One major factor? The "Sell in May and Go Away" proponents seem to ignore dividends[8] when comparing Treasuries' returns during the "Go Away" period to the total returns of stocks. Because stocks do pay dividends, even in the worst of times, they must be included in a fair analysis of the strategy. As is often the case, even the most cursory examination of a market "rule of thumb" will often disprove or greatly diminish its actual probability of success.

Misunderstanding #6—Believing Financial News Is Actionable

Stupid is as stupid does.

—Forrest Gump

The overwhelming majority of financial news is just noise. Part of being a successful investor is filtering out the noise as much as possible. A great example of this is how financial media will create, often out of thin air, an explanation for minor market movements.

For example, if the Dow is at 26,000 and closes the day up 100 points, it may sound like a decent-sized move, but it's not. It is a move of just .004 or a little more of one-third of 1 percent. This sort of move is usual, expected, and occurs because nothing substantive has happened. Nonetheless, the financial media needs to report on the day and will create a headline to

---

[8]Why is it that those who want to scare people out of the market or promote market timing leave out dividends? All that matters with any investment is the total return, which is capital appreciation *plus* dividends or income.

explain the change. They will select from any of the day's announcements and backfill a headline. For example, a headline might read "Stocks Up on Housing Report" or "Stocks Up on Middle East Talks." If the move is just 100 points, there is actually no explanation needed.

Let's say you run a chain of sandwich shops, and you sell an average of 26,000 sandwiches per day. Now, let's say that today you sold 26,100. Is there a reason? Are you going to examine all the things you did right today to sell 100 more sandwiches, or do you consider it perfectly normal variance? If, instead, you sell 25,900 sandwiches, are you going to look for the reasons why? Perhaps someone should be fired? Maybe you should remodel the stores? Of course not, because selling 100 sandwiches more or less on any given day is perfectly normal. In fact, selling 200 sandwiches more or less on any given day is also perfectly normal and would not cause you to blink, even for a moment.

Now, if you sell a thousand (more or less) sandwiches, perhaps something else is going on that merits investigation. It's the same with the stock market. The reality is that most market movements require no explanation. They just happen. The market doesn't close precisely where it opened very often, just like a chain of sandwich shops that sells an average of 26,000 sandwiches a day rarely actually sells that many on any given day. It's almost always more or less.

Just for fun, read the headlines on your favorite financial media site at the end of the day, and watch how they will often backfill a headline to explain statistically insignificant moves in the market. They have no choice. Can you imagine logging on to see CNBC and reading the headline "Nothing Big Happened Today; Check Back Tomorrow"?

Misunderstanding #7—Believing Republicans Are Better for the Market Than Democrats

The common viewpoint is that Republicans are good for . . . the economy. Meanwhile, the common view of Democrat policies is that they . . . are economy killers. Well, for those who feel this way, it may be time to review . . . economic history.

—Adam Hartung, *Forbes* (2012)

Most investors equate a Democratic victory as synonymous with a stock market downturn. History tells quite a different story. The markets are about as politically neutral as can be, with the broad market index up an average of 49% during Republican administrations versus an average of 46% during Democrat administrations. Even Congressional control by one party or the other doesn't significantly skew the results, as seen in the chart below:

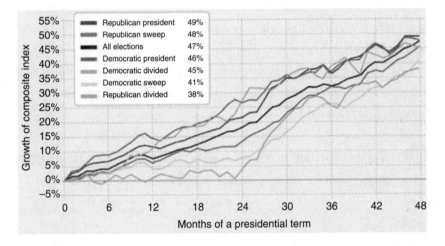

There are two main theories for this traditionally unexpected result. The first theory is that investors expect radical changes from Democratic presidents, including significantly higher taxes on income and investments, corporate taxes, and an environment generally less friendly toward corporations. The same theory holds that investors expect tax cuts, spending cuts, and fiscal restraint from Republican presidents. The stock market adjusts in advance of the expected outcome of the election. When a Democrat replaces a Republican, the market often adjusts upward when it realizes that the new president may be friendlier than originally expected toward corporations and high-income taxpayers. Likewise, the market often adjusts downward when it realizes that the new Republican president may not cut spending as expected. Proponents of this theory typically cite two examples: (1) tax cuts, free trade, and record surpluses under President Clinton and (2) record spending and deficits under President George W. Bush. The point is that the market has certain expectations from each party, and many times those expectations are not fulfilled, for whatever reason. The second theory is that this statistic is irrelevant and has more to do with the "luck of the draw" than with whoever is President (much in the same way the stock market tends to go up if the AFC wins the Super Bowl and decline if the NFC wins).

We do know with certainty that the market is continuously "pricing in" hundreds of variables—from the deficit to interest rates; the business cycle to commodity prices; from consumer confidence to corporate profits; and yes, whoever controls the White House and Congress.

As a result, we cannot emphasize one factor alone as having such a significant impact on stock market performance. In total, an election itself will not drive the markets.

Misunderstanding #8—Overestimating the Impact of a Manager

Among the smaller duties of life, I hardly know any one more important than that of not praising where praise is not due.

—Sydney Smith

The asset class selection is responsible for 88 percent of an investor's return, yet investors tend to give the most credit or blame to the asset manager for performance (see Figure 3.1).

FIGURE 3.1

Percentage of a portfolio's movements over time explained by:

Security selection and market timing   12%

Asset allocation   88%

Sources: The Vanguard Group, Inc. 2013. "Vanguard's Principles for Investing Success." The Vanguard Group; Using data from Morningstar.

In any given year, the top-performing and worst-performing funds tend to be in the same category. For example, in 2017, emerging markets funds were some of the top performers. Were the fund managers geniuses? No. The emerging markets index outperformed most of them. They simply happened to manage emerging markets funds in a year when the asset class did well. That same group performed quite poorly the next year when emerging markets were hammered. Were the same managers complete idiots? No. They just happened to manage emerging markets funds in a year when this asset class underperformed other areas of the market.

The reality is that when looking at performance, an investor must remember two important things: (1) Regardless of how the manager performed, the odds are very high they will lose to the index going forward, and (2) even if the performance is excellent, most of the return is indicative of how the asset class performed, rather than due to the manager's skill. The manager, for the most part, is along for the ride.

Misunderstanding #9—Believing Market Drops Are the Time to Get Defensive

The stock market is the only thing people prefer not to buy when it is on sale.
—Origin Unknown

When the market is dropping, all of the powerful forces we cover in this book, from the media to your behavioral instincts, will encourage you to take action to protect your portfolio. This usually means "getting defensive" by going to cash or switching your allocation, which is often a monumental mistake—one of the worst an investor can make. As we covered exhaustively in Chapter 1, this strategy does not work and causes more harm than good. Your reaction to a market drop should be the exact opposite. If you like the market at 26,000, you should love it at 20,000.

Your asset allocation should be a function of your goals. If 60 percent of your portfolio is in stocks, and the market drops 20 percent, you should buy more stocks to get your portfolio back to its target allocation. Selling stocks is abandoning the plan at the worst possible time.

Stocks seem to be the one thing that no one wants to buy when they are on sale. If your favorite restaurant offers everything at half off, you will eat there more. If your favorite car is for sale for half off, you will quickly buy one. If a grocery store cut the price of everything by 50 percent, you would go on a shopping spree. Yet when stock prices are cut in half, investors freeze and do nothing, or even worse, sell. Instead, they wait for the prices to double, and then they want to buy! Ignore all the prognosticators who are tempting and even encouraging you to panic and make a poor decision. Remember, everything is on sale. The time to buy is now.

Avoiding Mistake #3—Misunderstanding Performance and Financial Information

The greatest enemy of knowledge is not ignorance; it is the illusion of knowledge.
—Daniel J. Boorstin, *The Discoverers:*
A History of Man's Search to Know His World and Himself

A large part of the financial information an investor encounters is worthless, damaging, or misleading. For investors to protect themselves from taking action based on this sort of information, they must understand how reference sets work, understand that performance data can be misleading, view financial news with skepticism, and most importantly, *develop a skill for filtering out the noise.*

Letting Yourself Get in the Way

The most important quality for an investor is temperament, not intellect.

—Warren Buffett

Most people who get excited about investing dive into research, read market timing or stock pick letters, use online services, and watch financial news all the time. The idea is that the more they know, the better informed they will become, and the less likely they will be to make a mistake. It doesn't really work out this way. If you have a reasonable intelligence level and understand the basic principles of this book, you will likely outperform the great majority of investors. The key is not to mess things up. Unfortunately, there are plenty of ways to do just that. So far, we have examined strategies that are likely to do far more harm than good. But I have personally seen nothing cause more financial destruction than the emotionally driven mistakes investors make. The key is to recognize your behavioral biases so that you can knowingly protect yourself from making mistakes. Let's dive in.

Fear, Greed, and Herding

Fear has a greater grasp on human action than does the impressive weight of historical evidence.

—Jeremy Siegel

The fact that people will be full of greed, fear, or folly is predictable. The sequence is not predictable.

—Warren Buffett

A typical year in the market (see Figure 4.1) . . .

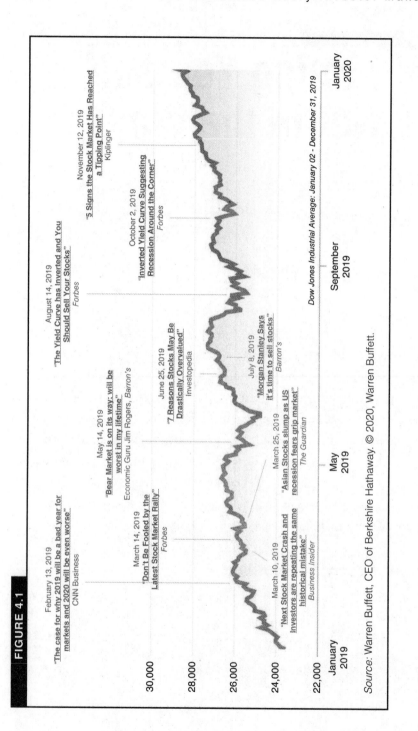

FIGURE 4.1

February 13, 2019
"The case for why 2019 will be a bad year for
markets and 2020 will be even worse"
CNN Business

March 14, 2019
"Don't Be Fooled by the
Latest Stock Market Rally"
Forbes

March 10, 2019
"Next Stock Market Crash and
investors are repeating the same
historical mistake"
Business Insider

May 14, 2019
"Bear Market is on its way: will be
worst in my lifetime"
Economic Guru Jim Rogers, Barron's

March 25, 2019
"Asian Stocks slump as US
recession fears grip market"
The Guardian

June 25, 2019
"7 Reasons Stocks May Be
Drastically Overvalued"
Investopedia

July 8, 2019
"Morgan Stanley Says
it's time to sell stocks"
Barron's

August 14, 2019
"The Yield Curve has Inverted and You
Should Sell Your Stocks"
Forbes

October 2, 2019
"Inverted Yield Curve Suggesting
Recession Around the Corner"
Forbes

November 12, 2019
"5 Signs the Stock Market Has Reached
a Tipping Point"
Kiplinger

30,000

28,000

26,000

24,000

22,000

January
2019

May
2019

September
2019

January
2020

Dow Jones Industrial Average: January 02 - December 31, 2019

Source: Warren Buffett, CEO of Berkshire Hathaway. © 2020, Warren Buffett.

As humans, fear and greed are two of our ugliest traits and most potent forces. They can impact the way we live our lives, and they can have very negative consequences for investors. Novice investors fall prey to it, legendary investors know how to control it, and the media and market prognosticators feed into it. Those two emotions, combined with our natural bias toward herding, can cause significant investment mistakes. Humans are hardwired to move in herds, follow the crowd, and to find safety in consensus. If the market is going down and the media, commentators, and our friends are yelling "head for the exits," our herding instinct, coupled with the powerful force of fear, is to do the same. If the market is rallying, and everyone is saying "full steam ahead," our herding instinct, coupled with the alluring force of greed, entices us to join the crowd.

The herding instinct can be very costly. From 1984 to 1995, the S&P 500 was up 15.4 percent per year, and the average mutual fund was up 12.3 percent per year. Over the same period, though, the average investor was up only 6.3 percent. Why? Because investors exit underperforming markets and buy into other markets that are doing well, always herding into the wrong place at the wrong time. This is what happens in nearly every significant bull and bear market (see Figure 4.2).

FIGURE 4.2

	Date	Equity Weighting	Investor Cash Flows over the Prior Two Years (in millions)		Stock Market Performance (cumulative)	
			Stock Funds	Bond Funds	Prior Two Years	Subsequent Two Years
Early in 1990s bull market	1/31/1993	34%	—	—	—	—
Bull market peak	3/31/2000	62	$393,225	$5,100	41%	−23%
Bear market bottom	2/28/2003	40	71,815	221,475	−29	53
Bull market peak	10/31/2007	62	424,193	173,907	34	−29
Bear market bottom	2/28/2009	37	−49,942*	83,921*	−51*	94

Sources: The Vanguard Group, Inc. 2013. "Vanguard's Principles for Investing Success."; Morningstar for equity, allocation, and cash flow data; Thomson Reuters datastream for market returns.

Unfortunately, these instincts cause the investor irreparable damage. Despite the market's insistence on going up for over 100 years, investors consistently mess up the inevitable gains by falling prey to some of the most powerful forces of human nature. In bear markets, investors have been mostly sellers when, in fact, had they only done nothing, they would have had substantial gains, regardless of when they bought. A more sophisticated investor is better served to take the opportunity to buy more, a strategy often referred to as opportunistic rebalancing. During substantial market drops, the smart investor is selling off bonds and buying stocks. With patience, this strategy has put the investor in a better place every time. Warren Buffett has historically held his positions and aggressively added during periods of investor hysteria. He has said to "be fearful when others are greedy and greedy when others are fearful." His words are gospel for the investor trying to control the seductive pulls of fear, greed, and herding.

In a 2014 interview, former Federal Reserve Chairman Alan Greenspan reflected back on all he had learned. Interestingly, rather than lots of economic analysis, he shared his observations of human behavior, saying:

> If you can grit your teeth through and just disregard short-term declines in the market or even long-term declines in the market, you will come out well. I mean you just stick all your money in stocks and go home and don't look at your portfolio you'll do far better than if you try to trade it. The reason that's the case is this asymmetry between fear and euphoria.[1] The most successful stock market players, the best investors, are those who recognize that the asymmetric bias in fear vs. euphoria is a tradable concept and can't fail for precisely this reason. So there are stabilities here which are very important, but along with them are more junk statistics, more junk analysis, and more stock market letters than should be allowed to be written. It's just sort of ridiculous. (Fox 2014)

---

[1] Mr. Fancy Pants is using the word "euphoria" in place of "greed." Same idea.

Interestingly, throughout his entire career, Greenspan essentially learned that almost everything is noise, and the strongest distinction he found among those who performed the best was that they were never scared into selling and embraced the opportunity to buy when others were fearful. Greenspan is endorsing only one tradable concept: the fear and greed trade. Control your fear, control your greed, avoid the herd, and things will work out. That's some pretty fascinating insight from the person most people considered the most powerful person on earth for much of his tenure.

Dr. Frank Murtha, a co-founder of MarketPsych, a behavioral economics consulting firm, said, "Investing is stressful, and that stress causes us to make emotional—usually fear-based—decisions during difficult market periods." He goes on to say that fear-based decisions impede reaching financial goals because they are focused on emotional, not financial needs, namely the desire "to feel in control again" (Fidelity Viewpoints 2013). Few things scare investors more than watching their portfolios go down day after day, week after week, and month after month. When we look back on corrections and bear markets with charts, they don't look so bad. But living through them is an entirely different story. The lack of control, the idea that the portfolio is deteriorating, and one can't do anything about it, causes investors to panic and sell. Selling makes them feel like they are in control again, yet the reality is quite the opposite. The market just kicked their butts. If you do this over and over, you will lose the game.

Rather than be fearful and sell out at the worst time or get greedy when the market is way up, investors should control their emotions and not only avoid panic but embrace the market volatility for what it is: *an opportunity and a gift*. Suffocate the instincts that want to make you a bad investor and embrace the chaos that causes them to rise to the surface.

The Overconfidence Effect

Nothing is so difficult as not deceiving oneself.

—Ludwig Wittgenstein

The overconfidence effect is a well-established bias in which someone's confidence in their judgments is greater than the reality, especially when confidence is relatively high. Let's be clear, though: there's nothing wrong with confidence in your abilities. Your mom wants you to be confident, your coach wants you to be confident, and I want you to be confident. Overconfidence, however, is quite dangerous as it means you are overestimating your ability to get something right. This can result in some relatively poor decision making in life and investing.

In his book, *The Psychology of Judgment and Decision Making*, Scott Plous said, "No problem in judgment and decision making is more prevalent and more potentially catastrophic than overconfidence" (Plous 1993, 217). It has been blamed for lawsuits, strikes, wars, and stock market bubbles and crashes. No, he isn't exaggerating.

Psychologists Marc Alpert and Howard Raiffa conducted various studies asking individuals a myriad of questions; for example, how many foreign automobiles were imported in the United States, how many physicians were listed in Boston's phone directory, and so on. The participants were told they could answer the question with as broad a range as they like, such as 1 to 1,000,000, but the range could be no more than 2 percent off. Across the studies, participants averaged an inaccuracy rate of over 40 percent. Alpert and Raiffa dubbed this interesting bias of individuals to overestimate their abilities the "overconfidence effect" (Alpert and Raiffa 1982). Since then, behavioral scientists have had a field day with the concept.

We now know that when someone says they are "99 percent sure," they are actually correct about 80 percent of the time (Kahneman and Lovallo 1993). People say they are "99 percent sure" all the time. Keeping in mind how accurate they probably are when they say that can help you make better decisions and make life more entertaining.[2] Study after study

---

[2] Is your spouse 99% sure he packed the keys to the condo? Is your son 99% sure he took out the trash? Are you 99% sure you paid that bill? I'm 99% sure there are few things as fun as knowing that when someone says that they are 99% sure of something, we know the odds they are right are 80%. Keep that in mind the next time you are parachuting, and someone tells you they are 99% sure they packed the parachute correctly.

bears out the enormous impact of the overconfidence effect: 93 percent of student drivers said their driving was above average (Svenson 1981), 94 percent of college professors think they are above-average (Cross 1977), most people think they are aboveaverage lovers[3] (Taleb 2007), and 85 percent of people believe their future will be more pleasant and less painful for them than the average person[4] (Armor and Taylor 2002). My favorite, though, is the study of students asked about their character: 79 percent said their character was better than most, despite 27 percent of them having stolen something from a store and 60 percent of them cheating on an exam in the previous year (Crary 2008).

The overconfidence effect has been studied and documented in the investment world more than any other area. Finance professors Brad Barber and Terrance Odean conducted a study comparing men's investment performance to women's (Barber and Odean 2001). They examined the trading patterns of 35,000 households over five years. They found that men's overconfidence in their abilities resulted in 45 percent more trading activity than women. And what exactly did all of this overconfidence get them? The trading *reduced* their average return by 2.65 percent per year, far underperforming the women. On top of that, the men paid more in transaction fees and taxes. Overconfidence can be very expensive.

In another study, a researcher found that when analysts are 80 percent certain a stock will go up, they are right just 40 percent of the time (Van Eaton 2000). In a 2006 study, researcher James Montier surveyed 300 professional fund managers asking them to rate their performance (Montier 2006). A full 74 percent of the managers surveyed said they had delivered above-average job performance (Montier 2006, 3). Zacharakis and Shepherd found that venture capitalists are wildly overconfident with their thoughts on the prospects of success for companies they invest in. The study found 96 percent of the venture capitalists exhibiting overconfidence (Zacharakis and Shepherd 2001). In other words, investment

---

[3]Admit it, you are pretty proud of yourself. ☺
[4]At least we are an upbeat bunch.

professionals, as a group, are frightfully wrong at what they are supposed to do best: Measure the likelihood of a particular outcome.

Richards Heuer researched the behavioral biases of CIA analysts. A key finding of his research is fascinating: "Once an experienced analyst has the minimum information necessary to make an informed judgment, obtaining additional information generally does not improve the accuracy of his or her estimates. *The additional information does, however, lead the analyst to be more confident in the judgment, to the point of overconfidence* [emphasis added]" (Heuer 1999, p. 52).

In a study on this effect, in conjunction with the Oregon Research Institute, Paul Slovic studied the impact of giving additional information to individuals handicapping a horse race. First, they gave each individual five important pieces of information and asked for their predictions. Then they gave them each an additional 35 pieces of information. *When Slovic asked for their predictions, the handicappers were less accurate but twice as confident* (Slovic 1973)!

The impact of additional information on investing is quite similar. We know that those who gather more information feel better about their investments and trade more, and we know that those who trade more underperform more. The investor is mistaking all of the additional information they are collecting as added intelligence to enable them to trade to their advantage. Instead, the studies bear out that the added information results in overconfidence. The overconfidence results in activity in the account that is a waste of a bunch of time, money, effort, and stress—all to create underperformance.

Before you think you are too smart to fall victim to the overconfidence effect, note that Scott Plous' research has found no link whatsoever between intelligence (or lack thereof) and overconfidence (Plous 1993). In fact, there is substantial evidence that the more intelligent people are, the more likely they are to be overconfident. Research shows physicians, lawyers, engineers, and entrepreneurs all exhibit overconfidence in their respective fields. For example, physicians routinely overestimate their ability to detect certain diseases (Christensen–Szalanski and Bushyhead 1981). Lawyers in civil cases consistently overestimate the frequency with which their side will prevail (Wagenaar and Keren 1986). Professionals also bring this overconfidence into the investment world, where they make mistakes and underperform (Daniel, Hirshleifer, and Subrahmanyam 1998; Odean 1998).

Overconfidence can take down the most sophisticated of investors. In 2011, MF Global, a brokerage and trading company, became one of the largest bankruptcies in history after a massive bet on European debt didn't work out. The cause of the collapse was attributed almost entirely to the overconfidence of its CEO, Jon Corzine, a former governor and Goldman Sachs chairman, and his team of traders. In 2012, JP Morgan, one of the world's largest investment banks, shook the markets when its traders created $2 billion of losses with a trading strategy run amok. Congress, concerned this signaled another 2008 crisis in the making, hauled JP Morgan's CEO, Jamie Dimon, in for Congressional hearings. The purpose of the hearings was to determine the cause of the market turmoil to prevent it from happening again. Members of the Senate expected to learn about complex trading algorithms, derivatives, or computer malfunctions. Instead, Dimon testified that the trading loss was attributable to "complacency" that led to "overconfidence" (Kopecki, Benson, and Mattingly 2012).

When you hear someone make a big, bold market prediction, it is usually accompanied by a large dose of overconfidence. There are too many variables to predict short-term market movements, and anyone knowledgeable about markets would never make a bold, short-term prediction. The bolder the call, the less valid the opinion.

Confirmation Bias

All can foresee the future only when it coincides with their own wishes, and the most grossly obvious facts can be ignored when they are unwelcome.

—George Orwell

Confirmation bias is the tendency for people to look for and favor information that confirms their preconceptions and beliefs and to avoid, devalue, or dismiss information that conflicts with their beliefs.

For example, a conservative may read the *Wall Street Journal*, view the Drudge Report online, and watch FOX News, while a liberal may read the *New York Times*, view the *Huffington Post* online, and watch MSNBC. Both seek out information that usually confirms their ideas and avoid information that may conflict with their ideas. When was the last time you subscribed to a magazine, bought a book, or regularly listened to or watched a political pundit who challenged your views? If you are like most people, it's been a long time. In fact, you probably spend most of your time validating what you think is right.

What if I asked you to write down your top 10 beliefs on hot political and religious topics? Think of things that tend to get people worked up: guns, abortion, fiscal policy, global warming, religious beliefs, and so on. Now, do you think you are right about all ten beliefs? If I brought to you the most prestigious and authoritative people in the world on each of the ten topics to present their thoughts to you, do you think any of your thoughts or ideas would change? They likely wouldn't. Instead, you would likely devalue or dismiss nearly everything they would have to say.

You see, we all think we are right—and not just about some things, about everything! And we continuously seek ways to validate what we think. *More knowledgeable people are doing just the opposite and instead are actively seeking out opposing views, challenging their ideas, and even occasionally changing their minds.*[5]

To better control this powerful force called confirmation bias, you need to recognize the little devil inside your brain constantly encouraging you to validate your preconceived ideas. If you can't do that in life, well, maybe you can at least try to control confirmation bias when it comes to investing.

There is ample evidence that confirmation bias permeates throughout investors' decisions. For example, once an investor likes a stock, he is likely to seek out information that validates the stock. In a 2010 study, researchers showed that investors used message boards to seek out

---

[5]When was the last time you changed your point of view on any major topic? Be honest with yourself.

information that validated, rather than challenged, stocks they owned (Park et al. 2010). If we own a stock, we tend to look for anything that validates our decision to buy it and reinforce why we should keep holding it.

Even Warren Buffett said that he finds himself falling prey to confirmation bias and actively seeks out other investors who disagree staunchly with his ideas. One way to deal with confirmation bias is to ask yourself everything that can go wrong. For example, if you like the idea of investing in a specific investment, pretend ten years has passed and that you have lost a substantial sum of money on it. Ask yourself all the ways that might have happened: force your brain to go through the exercise of acknowledging or even, dare I say, welcoming adverse ideas.

Anchoring

The anchoring heuristic appears to be prevalent throughout human decision processes . . .

—McElroy and Dowd (2007, p. 48)

In the 1970s, psychologists Daniel Kahneman and Amos Tversky identified the "anchoring" effect. Kahneman went on to win the 2002 Nobel Prize in economics. Tversky, who died in 1996, would have shared the prize. Their research opened the floodgates on a human bias that impacts all sorts of decision making.

Anchoring is a term psychologists use to explain how the brain takes mental shortcuts to arrive at conclusions. In short, there is a tendency for us to over-rely on the first piece of information that enters our brain. This piece of information is the "anchor." Once the anchor is set, all future decisions revolve around the anchor, contaminating rational thinking. If you are not sure of a correct answer, you will most likely fall victim to the anchoring bias and guess an answer based on the most recent information. For example, if asked whether Zimbabwe's population is more or less than 20 million, you will give an answer. Then, if asked what you think is the actual population, you will likely answer somewhat close to 20 million.

Anchoring is well known by both novice and experienced nego-
tiators. The first price thrown out in a negotiation often becomes the
anchor. Marketers have seized upon the anchoring bias. You encounter
it every time you go to the grocery store. In a fascinating experiment,[6]
Wansink, Kent, and Hoch (1998, pp. 74–75) set up a display with Campbell's Soup on sale for 79 cents per can with a sign that said, "No Limit."
They then added a sign that said, "Limit of 12 per person." The shoppers who purchased the soup on sale without a limit bought an average
of 3.3 cans. The shoppers who purchased the soup on sale for the same
price, but with a limit of 12, purchased seven cans. The shoppers were
anchored to the number 12, assigning some meaning to it (for example,
"Wow, this must be a terrific deal, and the grocery store doesn't want me
to buy a lot or they'll lose money."). There are many, many more studies
on the anchoring effect. It is real, it is vivid, and many of us have been
unknowing victims of it for years!

But wait, this is a book on investing. I'm sure you know where I am
going, though! The anchoring effect with stock purchases is often, you
guessed it, your purchase price. If you purchase a stock for $50 and it
is later $30, you may hold onto it until it gets back to $50, or even buy
more because you think it is worth $50. If instead, the stock goes from
$50 to $70, you may sell the stock thinking it is overvalued because
the price is so much higher than $50. The anchor clouds your decision
making. Many investors fall victim to anchoring by buying a stock that
has come far off its highs ("It's a bargain now!"), or not purchase a stock
that has run on to new highs ("It is too overpriced now!"). The reality is
often, in both cases, that the stock is priced pretty darn close to where it
should be, with an equal number of buyers on one side and sellers on the
other. The only reason the investor thinks it is a great bargain or overpriced is its direction from its past "anchor" price. With a heightened
sense of awareness of the anchoring bias, you can avoid holding losers
too long and selling winners too early. And maybe you can save some
money at the grocery store.

---

[6] I have been told I am easily fascinated.

Loss Aversion

Having a long-term plan—and not casting it aside—is the key to dealing with our fear of loss (loss aversion).

—Ori Brafman and Rom Brafman
Sway: The Irresistible Pull of Irrational Behavior

Kahneman and Tversky are also heralded for their research regarding another powerful human bias, which they coined "loss aversion." Loss aversion is the stronger bias humans have to avoid a loss rather than make a gain. In other words, we fear losing more than we enjoy winning. Losses hurt more than the pleasure we get from gains.

Extensive research that has followed Kahneman and Tversky's studies show us that humans experience about twice as much pain from a loss as the pleasure they receive from gains.

In one study, researchers gave one group of people a pen with a $3.98 price sticker on it (Kahneman, Knetsch, and Thaler 1991). They then asked a group without the pens how much they would pay to purchase a pen and asked the group with pens how much they would require to sell their pen. Those who didn't have the pens valued the pens at a much lower amount than those who did. Why is this? Because those who already had a pen didn't want to "lose" by selling it for less than $3.98, and those who did not have a pen didn't want to "lose" by paying $3.98 or more.

Have you been to a jewelry store lately? Have you noticed how they try to put the jewelry in your hands or try to get you to wear it? They are well aware of how loss aversion works. In this form of loss aversion, known as the "endowment effect" or "status quo effect," once you have a pen, jewelry, or whatever in your hands, it feels like it's yours, and you don't want to lose it.[7]

Loss aversion in all of its forms perhaps causes more damage among investors than any other group. Loss aversion is why investors sit in cash,

---

[7]"Let's see if this necklace fits you." "I bet this blouse would look lovely on you. Let's try it on." "How about we take the car for a test drive?"

despite knowing full well that they are purposefully and willfully losing the purchasing power of their money. The average money market yield has been well below inflation for decades. Despite that fact, investors are willingly losing a little each day to avoid potential losses with real investments. With a plan like this, purchasing power can be cut in half in just 24 years!

Loss aversion is the reason you won't finally give away the pair of pants that haven't fit you since 1994, the sweater that you haven't worn since 2003, and the reason you won't give away all the stuff you never use that you have accumulated in your garage, attic, and every other crevice of storage space in your house. Let it go. Move on!

Loss aversion is the reason that you hang on to a stock long after it has dropped. You don't want to acknowledge the loss, which would require you to no longer deny you made a mistake. Far better to just wait until it (maybe) recovers, right? Whenever I am talking with a client who has an investment they won't sell until it recovers, I ask them a simple question: "If you had the cash instead of this stock, knowing what you are trying to accomplish, would you buy the same stock today?" The answer is almost always no, and when it is, we know the investor is hanging on only because of the loss aversion effect. Simple awareness of how our mind works and understanding the impact of loss aversion on our decision making can help us become better investors.[8]

Mental Accounting

Since the conscious mind can only handle a few thoughts at any given time, it's constantly trying to "chunk" stuff together to make the complexity of life a little more manageable. Instead of counting every dollar we spend, we parcel our dollars into particular purchases. We rely on misleading shortcuts because we lack the computational power to think any other way.

—Jonah Lehrer, Wired.com

Richard Thaler is known for his work in the field of behavioral economics, and for identifying and defining *mental accounting*. Through

---

[8]And make us less likely to clutter our way onto the next episode of Hoarders!

mental accounting, an individual will divide their current and future assets into separate, nontransferable portions.

For example, in a study highlighting the impact of mental accounting (Kahneman and Tversky 1984, 347–348), participants were asked the following:

Imagine that you have decided to see a movie and have paid the admission price of $10 per ticket. As you enter the theater, you discover that you have lost the ticket. The ticket cannot be recovered. Would you pay $10 for another ticket? Only 46 percent of the participants said they would purchase another ticket. He then asked the participants a similar question: Imagine that you have decided to see a movie where admission is $10 per ticket. As you enter the theater, you discover that you have lost a $10 bill. Would you still pay $10 for a ticket to the movie? Even though the economic impact was precisely the same as with the first question, 88 percent of the participants said yes, they would buy a ticket!

Under both scenarios, a participant was asked to spend $10 on a ticket, despite losing $10 earlier. The difference in the responses is attributable to the powerful effect of mental accounting. Once participants had a ticket, they assigned it to the "entertainment" column of their mental account. They had already lost their budget for the movie, so they weren't going to go over budget and buy another ticket. The latter group lost $10, not a ticket for which they paid $10. This group had not yet assigned the $10 to the ticket, and therefore was willing to purchase a ticket. The study shows that we don't view every dollar the same, even though we obviously should.

Psychologist Hal Arkes' research shows us that mental accounting is why tax refunds and lottery winnings are often blown quickly (Arkes et al. 1994). Mental accounting puts them in the "free money" column even though we all know a dollar is really just a dollar!

Sociologist Viviana Zelizer, referencing a study on the Oslo prostitution market, notes that the principle even applies to how those in the world's oldest profession spend their income (Zelizer 1994, p. 3). The prostitutes in the study used their welfare checks and health benefits to pay rent and other bills and used the money they acquired selling sex on drugs and alcohol. Mental accounting is ingrained in the human condition.

If you have ever gambled and found yourself winning, you may notice you became more aggressive when playing with "house money." Again, the mental accounting effect is at work. Money is money; we just account for it differently because of our human biases. Mental accounting impacts how we make decisions in everyday life and contributes to wealth destruction among investors who fall into its trap. If an investor looks at each investment separately, he is creating separate mental accounts for each holding. By doing this, the investor is far more likely to hold onto losers in any account with a loss than to wait for it to break even and to sell off winners in the accounts with gains to "lock it in."

If you hold separate investment accounts, keep in mind that they should not be judged individually, but rather as to whether they contribute appropriately to your long-term objective. Looking at the "big picture," it is far easier to judge if you are on track for your long-term goals. Looking at each holding or subaccount piecemeal can result in mental accounting that can trigger poor decision making. One way to dampen the impact of mental accounting in investing is to aggregate as many of your investments as possible into one account. Doing so makes it far easier to make overall decisions that make sense for you and dampens the mental accounting effect.

Recency Bias

If only the past were prologue, it would be a great thing. Returns do not persist. Good markets turn to bad. Bad markets turn to good. So the system is almost rigged against human psychology. If something does well in the past, it will do well in the future—that is not true. It is categorically false.

—John Bogle

Investors project out into the future what they have most recently been seeing. That is their unshakable habit.

—Warren Buffett

Recency bias is the tendency to project one's most recent experiences or observations into the future. This mental shortcut lets us make predictions about what will happen in the future based on the recent past. The problem is this mental shortcut can create lots of problems for investors.

As humans, we are programmed to make it as easy as possible to make decisions. Most of the time, a pattern we see in the recent past will play out going forward. It worked great for the cavemen. If you see a saber-tooth tiger next to a particular cave three days in a row, it's probably best to avoid that cave! The world we live in also encourages recency bias in many ways.

The financial media have a chronic case of recency bias. Researchers reviewed *Fortune*, *Forbes*, and *Businessweek* cover stories on companies over 20 years, grouping the 549 cover stories into positive, neutral, and negative categories. Looking at the 500 days before each positive cover story, they found that the company featured outperformed the index by an average of 42.7 percent; those with negative coverage had underperformed by 34.6 percent. In the 500 days following the cover stories, the companies with a negative review outperformed by 12.4 percent, while those with a positive review outperformed by just 4.2 percent (Arnold, Earl, and North 2007).

The recency bias is a dangerous instinct when it comes to investing, and when not controlled, can be very costly. Studies show brokers tend to recommend hot stocks that have outperformed over the previous year and that those recommendations underperform the market in the following year. Investors tend to jump on stocks that have risen many months in a row, expecting the trend to continue.

The tech bubble and 9/11 bear markets were back to back, causing many investors to expect another bear market and miss the recovery. Likewise, the market went down almost constantly in late 2008 and 2009, causing many investors to expect recent events to continue. Exiting the market, the investors missed out on the inevitable recovery. Whenever the market appears calm and rises steadily, money pours in from the sidelines, eager to buy once things appear stable.

Of course, markets don't work like this. In any given year, the odds are high the market will positively end the year, regardless of what happened the year before. Also, in any given year, the odds are good there will be a correction, regardless of what happened in the prior weeks, months, or years. Finally, in any given decade, an investor can expect about two bear markets, regardless of what happened the previous decade.

Recency bias may have worked well for the caveman, and even today may help us with some of our daily activities. Investing is one area the recency bias causes harm, not good, and unfortunately, it is where its impact is most costly.

Bloomberg frequently asks strategists for their recommended allocation to stocks. Note in Figure 4.3 that the highest allocation to stocks was near the market peak in 2001, just before the Internet bubble burst. The lowest allocation to stocks was near the market low in 2009. These recommendations were a reflection of the analysts' thinking that recent events were likely to continue. In both cases, they were dramatically wrong, and in both cases, the damage to the portfolio of anyone following this advice was substantial. That's recency bias at work.

One useful tool to combat recency bias in investing is to follow a disciplined system for managing your money. For example, if you are in a portfolio of 70 percent stocks and 30 percent bonds, you might decide

FIGURE 4.3

Source: Graph from Wall Street Strategists Remain Bearish, 2012. © Bespoke Investment Group LLC.

to rebalance only when the allocation changes by more than 5 percent. Another system is to set trades according to a calendar. For example, suppose you are exiting a sizeable single stock position. In that case, you might exit one-fifth every month until it is diversified so that you don't get consumed with a new decision on whether to sell each month, a decision that would likely be impacted by recent events. With a system like this, your investment decisions will be based on your disciplined process rather than recent market events.

Negativity Bias

Brief contact with a cockroach will usually render a delicious meal inedible. The inverse phenomenon—rendering a pile of cockroaches on a platter edible by contact with one's favorite food—is unheard of.
—Paul Rozin and Edward Royzman, "Negativity Bias, Negativity Dominance, and Contagion" (2001)

Negativity bias is the nature of humans to recall negative experiences more vividly than positive ones, and therefore act consciously and subconsciously to avoid negative experiences.

The negativity bias certainly helped humans survive thousands of years ago. It made sense to remain vigilant to potential things that could kill you—you know, things like wild animals, crazy people with spears, and the like. Today, the negativity bias is a dead weight dragging the unsuspecting down.

The negativity bias is well documented as a powerful instinct. Teresa Amabile and Steven Kramer studied professionals' workdays and found that negative setbacks, even if minor, were twice as powerful in impacting happiness as positive steps forward (Amabile and Kramer 2011). Researchers have also observed that learning happens faster with negative reinforcement than positive reinforcement (Haizlip et al. 2012).[9] Analyzing language, researchers found that 62 percent of emotional words were negative, and 74 percent of words describing personality traits were

---

[9]Well, that's a bit depressing!

negative (Averill 1980). Research shows that negativity bias is inherent in young children, who perceive positive faces as good, negative faces as bad, and, surprisingly, neutral facial expressions as negative (Tottenham et al. 2013). Research tells us even babies have the negativity bias, almost proving we are "born with it" (Hamlin, Wynn, and Bloom 2010).

How many times have you left an encounter with someone wondering if that person was upset with you, only because they weren't smiling the entire time? The negativity bias even affects marriage. Research by John Gottmann shows that married couples have positive and negative interactions as we all do. For a marriage to last, however, the ratio is five positive interactions for each negative one. (Marano 2004) Such is the force of our negativity bias.[10]

Our negativity bias is why the news feeds us far more negative information than good ("3 dead in a heat wave!" as opposed to "Los Angeles posts best year of weather in 10 years!" or "Plane slides off runway in Chicago," instead of "There hasn't been a fatal plane crash in 3 years, a record for the industry."). It's also why during campaign season, a politician will spend far less time on his own positives and far more time on his opponent's negatives—he is feeding into our negativity bias, which resonates much louder.

For goodness sake, you must be saying, what does this have to do with investing? The negativity bias is well at work in the investment world. We know that investors feel the pain of losses twice as much as the pleasure of gains. This tilt toward the negative encourages investors suffering from negativity bias to sell during corrections—at precisely the wrong time. They would prefer to run to cash than experience the pain of the negative experience. The negativity bias is especially dangerous when there are recent events that make it more acute. This phenomenon is described by a behavioral science term called "vividness." Some investors ride through corrections just fine, but after going through a severe bear market, such as the 2008 and 2009 financial crisis, the vividness of that experience coupled with the negativity bias becomes too much for the investor to bear. At the slightest correction, he panics and sells at the

---

[10]Take a break and tell your spouse you love them!

wrong time. Vividness can create a trigger effect reaction among investors, even from the slightest market dip.

As with all behavioral biases, the best way to combat it is to be aware of it, recognize it, and squash it before the negativity bias negatively impacts you or your portfolio.

The Gambler

You've got to know when to hold 'em, know when to fold 'em, know when to walk away, know when to run.

—Kenny Rogers

We all have a gambler inside us; it's just a question of whether we can control him. Some of us are speculators, placing bets in the market and hoping for the best. Speculators include most people trading options, market timing, or placing bets on just one or two positions, all in the hope of hitting a home run or beating the market. Most of us like to think of ourselves as investors. We follow a disciplined, repeatable strategy focused on long-term investing to increase the probability of achieving our goals. Many of us, though, have a little speculating devil inside of us as well.

We all have a subconscious desire to gamble. That's why Las Vegas always finds a way to make money. Human psychology is such that if we are winning, our endorphins go crazy, and we keep playing because it *feels good*. Human psychology also encourages us to keep playing when we are losing. We keep playing for two reasons: We want to feel good again but also because we hate losing and desperately want to break even. Casinos know this, of course. They start with the odds in their favor, but our human biases encourage us to keep playing, whether we are winning or losing, making sure the house odds ultimately work out for the casino. You see, the odds of winning a hand at blackjack are around 49 percent. A casino can't stay in business if people bet a hand of blackjack once or twice. The casino would lose about half the time. But, if you play a few hundred hands of blackjack, the odds are overwhelmingly against you. When was the last time you played one or two hands of blackjack or any casino game?

The market is just as unforgiving. While the market itself goes up, the stocks within it can move all over the place, and as we know, most of the stocks underperform the market. Trading stocks also has a "house" or two that win every time: the brokerage house, which will collect a commission, and the IRS, which will collect taxes. The odds that an investor will win trading stocks is the same as that of a gambler winning at the tables in Las Vegas: less than 50 percent. And as with gambling, the more times an investor trades, the more likely the odds will catch up with him, and he will lose.

Have you ever noticed what your online trading platform looks and sounds like? It's green and red, with scrolling tickers, flashing images, and dinging sounds. Just like a casino. Do you think that is a coincidence?[11]

Avoiding Mistake #4—Letting Yourself Get in the Way

The human mind is complicated. We can't seem to shake many of the primal instincts that have been hardwired into us over thousands of years. Some of our biases can quickly take over, especially those that are instinctual like fear, greed, and herding. However, all of the behavioral finance biases we have gone over here are powerful and impact how amateurs and professionals invest.

Remember, the market has never taken a dollar from anyone. To lose money, you have to fall prey to one of the mistakes in this book. The top mistake people make? Letting themselves get in the way. Ultimately, it is our own behavior that does us in. The key to dodging this pitfall is to be aware of what your instincts are telling you and recognize the behavioral landmines we have covered in this chapter. Take a step back, slow down, and follow the disciplined plan you have laid out for you and your family. The car is going to get to its destination unless you personally drive it off the cliff.

---

[11]It's not.

Working with the Wrong Advisor

Many investors choose to work with a financial advisor. High-net-worth investors tend to use financial advisors more than the general population. There are many different theories as to why this may be the case. Many high-net-worth households have concluded any of the following:

- They have too much to lose by making a major mistake.
- They are more likely to benefit from even minor improvements of after-tax, after-cost results.
- They are more likely to substantially benefit from noninvestment planning advice.
- They are comfortable utilizing professionals and paying for advice.
- They value their time and don't want to spend it dealing with financial decisions.
- They want someone to serve as a resource to them or their family for ongoing issues.
- They want someone to provide continuity of advice in the event of incapacity or death.

Many Americans make the mistake of waiting until they have substantial assets and then look primarily for investment help. Laying out a comprehensive road map for success early on helps investors get on the right track, pointing all efforts in the right direction. While it is true that incremental benefits do not have as much of an impact on smaller portfolios, say someone with $100,000 to invest, having a strong advisor by your side can still make a big difference toward reaching your goals. Whether you want to utilize an advisor is up to you, of course, but if you are going to use one, beware of the pitfalls.

Most Advisors Will Do Far More Harm Than Good

If you can, help others; if you cannot do that, at least do no harm to them.
—Dalai Lama XIV

I'll let you in on a big financial services industry secret: Most advisors will do far more harm than good.

The vast majority of advisors fall into one of three camps:

1. They take custody of your money as part of the regular course of business.

2. They are salespeople in disguise.

3. They utilize strategies that cause more harm than good because they try to sell you something that you want to hear. They do this even though they know it won't work or don't know what they are doing.[1]

There are many things to look for in an advisor, but if you can navigate the three core issues of custody, conflict, and competence, you will eliminate about 90 percent of advisors, and your odds of ending up with someone competent who won't steal your money or work you over will be much higher.

Advisor Selection Issue #1—Custody

Brokerages and advisers should have independent custodians, and the government should have forced me to have an independent custodian. Client funds should be held by independent custodians. If they had, I would have been caught long ago. If I had had an inspection by the SEC, they would have looked at the custodian

---

[1] I am so not looking forward to the hate mail I will receive from some financial advisors, but so be it.

accounts and seen the funds on my books did not match the funds in the accounts, and I would have been caught.

—Bernie Madoff (Patel 2013)

In 2008, the Bernie Madoff scandal received an enormous amount of press coverage. For those not familiar with the scandal, Bernie Madoff, considered one of the nation's top money managers, admitted that he was running the biggest Ponzi scheme in history. He paid for client withdrawals out of money transferring in from new clients. The only reason Madoff was exposed is that he was faced with massive withdrawal requests from investors as the market plummeted. Because Madoff had spent or hidden most of his clients' money long ago, he didn't have any money to meet the new requests. With the stock market panic, the new deposits couldn't meet the demand for new withdrawals. With no new money left to hide the greatest financial fraud in history, Madoff confessed.

What Bernie Madoff did was despicable on a variety of levels. He not only stole money from the super-wealthy and celebrities, but he bankrupted the "millionaire next door" and robbed hundreds of millions of dollars from charities and foundations. René-Thierry Magon de La Villehuchet, a wealthy businessman who referred clients to Madoff, committed suicide from the shame of association. Many of Madoff's former clients sold their homes and personal belongings. Very high profile foundations lost most of their money, and some were even forced to shut down.

The media coverage reached a fever pitch, mainly because of the fraud's scale, and because Madoff was not the only money manager stealing from clients. It is estimated that the SEC is usually investigating several hundred possible Ponzi schemes at any given time. Ponzi schemes come to light most frequently during market crashes, like 2008/2009 (see Figure 5.1).

There are not more crooks during those periods; it is just easier for them to get caught. During bear markets, many investors panic and ask for their money back, but because the money has been stolen and spent, and no new money is coming in due to the shaky markets, the advisor

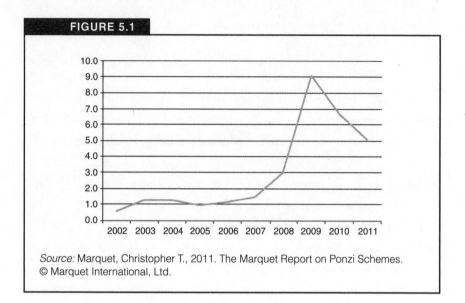

FIGURE 5.1

Source: Marquet, Christopher T., 2011. The Marquet Report on Ponzi Schemes.
© Marquet International, Ltd.

is unable to meet the withdrawal request and is exposed. As Warren Buffett said, "It is when the tide rolls out that we see who has been swimming naked."

Some people in the media have blamed the investors themselves for not investigating their advisor. Yet, how could an investor possibly have known what Bernie Madoff was doing? A background check would have shown a man who was a member of many exclusive clubs, served on the boards of charities and hospitals and was actively involved in his religious community and causes. He gave millions to various charities, and his clients included some of the world's most sophisticated investors. Madoff even served as the chairman of NASDAQ. Yes, there were red flags. A single accountant with two assistants audited his funds. His investment returns, up about 10 percent every year, did not behave the way returns work in the real world. Nevertheless, it is difficult to fault the investors.

The real issue is custody. When an investor speaks with their advisor, one of the top questions that should be asked is: "Who has custody of my money?" If a client hired Madoff, they wrote a check to "Madoff Investments," and the money was deposited in the Madoff Investments account. Therefore, Madoff had custody of his clients' assets. If he withdrew all the money from one investor's account and gave it to another investor making a withdrawal, no one would know the difference. Madoff's clients received reports created only by Madoff's firm, reflecting their returns (which, somehow, never went down).

The ideal way to work with an advisor is to have a separation of assets. For example, use an advisor who opens an account for you at a national brokerage firm. You can then sign a Limited Power of Attorney giving the advisor the right to place trades and bill the account only. The advisor should not have the authority to make other withdrawals. Furthermore, if your advisor provides reports to you, note that you should get the statement from the brokerage firm as well.

There are thousands of investment managers across the country advising clients in this manner, but many don't. For this reason, it would be imprudent for an investor to choose an advisor who insists on taking custody of all the client's investable assets.

To be clear, an advisor who uses a third-party custodian can still have various forms of legal custody. For example, if the advisor is also a law firm and serves as a trustee, a trustee by definition has custody. If you are working with a trust company, the trust company, by law, has custody. That is part of why you are hiring them—to entrust your funds with them rather than the beneficiary. Also, all advisors have custody to the extent that they can withdraw their fee from your account.

While we can slice and dice the custody rules, the point here is that your money should be held at a third party at all times. However, certain types of investments require that you give up custody of your money, which can make them attractive targets for Ponzi schemes. These include some hedge funds, private equity funds, and real estate funds (see Figure 5.2).

If you are not able to perform tremendous due diligence on these funds, ask yourself if you really need this type of investment. It is relatively common for a client to bring me a "deal" and tell me that they are comfortable giving up custody because the person running the

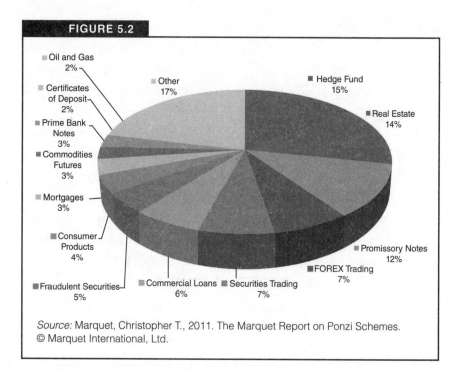

FIGURE 5.2

- Oil and Gas 2%
- Certificates of Deposit 2%
- Prime Bank Notes 3%
- Commodities Futures 3%
- Mortgages 3%
- Consumer Products 4%
- Fraudulent Securities 5%
- Commercial Loans 6%
- Securities Trading 7%
- FOREX Trading 7%
- Promissory Notes 12%
- Real Estate 14%
- Hedge Fund 15%
- Other 17%

Source: Marquet, Christopher T., 2011. The Marquet Report on Ponzi Schemes. © Marquet International, Ltd.

investment is at the same place of worship, is the same ethnicity, or the like. However, most Ponzi schemes (see Figure 5.3) are "affinity scams," that is, the promoter is preying on their own people, just like Madoff did.

The biggest mistake Madoff's investors made was not their failure to conduct a background check, as the media suggested. *The biggest mistake was giving him custody of all their money.* The first question you and your family should ask before entrusting everything you've worked for to an advisor is: "Who will take custody of my assets?" If the answer is the advisor, look elsewhere. If you get the right answer, *then* move on to the other essential issues of conflict and competence. If you don't want someone to be able to steal your money easily, don't give it to them. It's that simple. Also, don't give it to an advisor who will turn around and hand your money to hedge funds or other funds to take custody of your money. Many of Madoff's victims didn't hire Madoff directly but rather had paid advisors who in turn handed over custody of their money to Madoff.

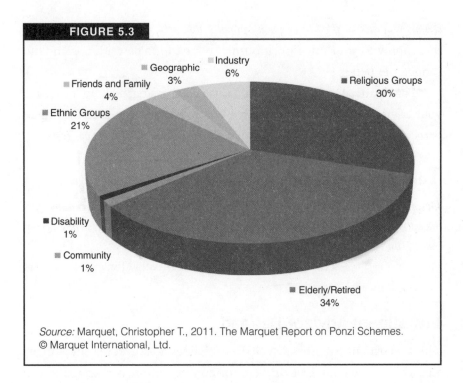

FIGURE 5.3

Source: Marquet, Christopher T., 2011. The Marquet Report on Ponzi Schemes.
© Marquet International, Ltd.

Advisor Selection Issue #2—Conflict

Conflict of Interest: A conflict between the private interests and the official responsibilities of a person in a position of trust.

—Merriam-Webster's Dictionary[2]

There are so many ways to get worked over by an advisor that it is, quite frankly, incredible. I am aware of no other industry where people go to a professional to get help and, more often than not, end up worse off than when they started. That's not a very nice thing to say, and it will ruffle the feathers of quite a few in the industry, but the reality is that the financial services industry is broken. If you have a typical advisor, the odds are you would be better off without one. The reason is simple: The overwhelming majority of advisors are not legally obligated to be on your side of the table at all times. *They get paid more if they sell you*

---

[2]For an example, see the financial services industry.

certain products, or they work for a company that sells its own funds. If any of these apply to your situation, it is time to look for a new advisor, and the sooner, the better.

The financial services landscape is very confusing, making it easy for your advisor to mislead you. Here, I will break out this issue into three parts to help you determine if your advisor passes these critical tests.

Test #1—Independent Advisor or Broker?

Despite what many consumers have been led to believe, not all financial advisors have their best interest in mind when suggesting investment vehicles. They do not practice under a fiduciary standard.

—The National Association of Personal Financial Planners

Investment Advisor Defined

The Investment Advisors Act of 1940 defines a "registered investment advisor" as "a person or firm that, for compensation, is engaged in the act of providing advice, making recommendations, issuing reports or furnishing analyses on securities, either directly or through publications." Advisors provide advice and recommendations and are paid a fee.

Investment advisors follow the fiduciary standard. *An investment advisor has a fiduciary duty to his or her clients, which means that they have a fundamental obligation to always act in the clients' best interests.* Investment advisors must disclose any and all conflicts of interest and are prohibited from engaging in trades for the sole purpose of creating more revenue for the advisor or their firm. Registered investment advisors are governed by the SEC or state-level equivalent.

Broker Defined

The Securities Exchange Act of 1934 defines a "broker" as "any person engaged in the business of effecting transactions in securities for the account of others." Brokers must register with FINRA.

In short, brokers are typically paid commissions tied to buying and selling investments that they select for their clients. As such, brokers were traditionally held to what was known as "the suitability standard," which meant that brokers did not have a legal obligation to always act in their client's best interests. Instead, the suitability standard says the broker must believe that any recommendations made are suitable for their clients. Under this standard, the act of selling you a product or fund that was more profitable to the broker—even if there were other products or funds with better performance or lower cost—was perfectly acceptable so long as the recommended product could be considered "suitable." The problem for consumers is that brokers often provide comparable services to investment advisors, but they aren't held to the same legal standard of care.

To improve the situation, the SEC introduced Regulation Best Interest (or Reg BI for short) in 2019. Reg BI states that brokers must be held to a higher standard when providing certain types of advice and must act in their clients' "best interest" in those circumstances. So, are all brokers now fiduciaries? The answer is a definitive no. The SEC has clarified that it sees the brokerage world and investment advisory world as different. Even under the new regulation, brokers are still permitted to "[offer] only proprietary products, placing material limitations on the menu of products, or incentivizing the sale of such products through its compensation practice" so long as these conflicts are disclosed to clients.[3]

So What's the Difference?

The bottom line is this: If your advisor is a registered investment advisor, the advisor serves as a fiduciary to you and is held to the highest legal standard of care. If your advisor is a broker, they are not. *Why in the world would you ever pay for advice from someone who isn't held to the highest legal standard of care?* To determine if the financial advisor is an investment advisor or broker, you will need to ask questions and investigate. It won't be easy because many advisors will try to mislead you. Brokers want to use titles that make them appear as if they are on your side of the table. They use titles like "financial advisor," "financial planner," "wealth advisor," and

---

[3]In long and complex legal documents they probably don't expect anyone to read.

"wealth manager." Brokers not only have no fiduciary duty, but they are also actively lobbying Congress to keep it that way. Keep that in mind.[4]

An independent investment advisor has a fiduciary duty to you and is subject to the highest legal standards of care; a broker does not. There are over 650,000 "financial advisors" in the United States. Most of them are brokers. That means most of the financial services industry isn't held to the highest legal standard of care when managing your money. Fascinating, right? Well, eliminate the brokers by asking a few questions:

1. Are you a broker or investment advisor? Correct answer: Investment advisor only.

2. Are you registered with the SEC or FINRA? Correct answer: SEC only, not both, and not just FINRA.

3. Do you have the Series 6, 7 or 65 license? Correct answer: The 65, not both, and not just the 6 or 7.

Note that all of the above are really the same question. An investment advisor never registered with FINRA. A broker will have the Series 7. We have narrowed the field by eliminating approximately 85 percent of the financial advisors. Let's narrow the field further[5] (PBS 2013).

Test #2—Pure Independent versus Independent and Broker

The dually registered advisor is the ultimate wolf in sheep's clothing.

---

[4]Imagine this: You pay a financial advisor and he shares the fee with his firm. That firm then spends some of that money lobbying Congress to allow them to advise you without having to act in your best interests. That sums up the majority of the financial services industry, and it's totally ridiculous.

[5]Note that I am not saying that all brokers are bad. That is certainly not the case. There are ethical and unethical brokers just like there are ethical and unethical investment advisors. I am simply saying that you should, at a minimum, require that the person you hire to help you is held to the highest legal standard of care at all times, and brokers don't meet that requirement.

So far, we have divided the financial advisory field into two main categories: independent investment advisors and brokers. However, we need to go one more step to make sure you are always dealing with someone that must *always* be held to the highest legal standard of care, not just some of the time. Some independent investment advisors are dually registered; they are both an independent advisor and a broker.

This advisor is dangerous because they can truthfully say that they are an investment advisor and held to the fiduciary standard. However—and this is a *huge* however—*the same person can switch from being an investment advisor with a fiduciary duty to act in your best interests, to a broker, without the obligation to act that way in the same conversation.* Yes, you read that right. By dually registering, an advisor can operate under the fiduciary standard sometimes and as a broker avoiding the standard in others. Good luck figuring out which is which. The dually registered advisor is the ultimate wolf in sheep's clothing.

There are two ways to see if an "independent investment advisor" is also operating as a broker. First, ask. Second, look at their business card or website. If it says, "securities offered by ABC broker-dealer," then you are dealing with someone who is also a broker. If you are working with a dually registered advisor, don't be surprised if your investment portfolio ends up owning commissionable investments or proprietary funds (funds that the company owns).

Test #3—Proprietary Funds versus No Proprietary Funds

It is improbable that your advisor happens to work for the one company that has the absolute best investment for you for any allocation in your portfolio.

Advisors who are brokers or are dually registered often work for a company whose parent company or sister company offers proprietary funds. That is, the company owns funds, and often it will sell those funds to its clients. For example, in a typical setup, an investment firm owns two sub-firms: a registered investment advisor (RIA) and a brokerage that owns mutual funds, hedge funds, and the like. The financial advisors are then dually registered. The advisors market themselves as "independent advisors." The client signs an agreement they never read or wouldn't understand anyway. The "independent advisor" then puts the sister company's mutual funds, separately managed accounts, and hedge funds into the client's portfolio. These funds often operate under different names, making it even harder for the client to know they are being sold proprietary funds. In my opinion, *this is the worst type of setup for a client because the client has gone through the effort to seek out an independent advisor and instead ended up with a salesperson in disguise.* And make no mistake, when you hire a broker, you are hiring a salesperson, not an advisor. If you are going to pay an advisor to give you advice, the least you should ask for is that they don't have a product to sell you and that they are held to the highest legal standard of care.

You don't go to a Honda dealership and pay someone to tell you what brand of car to buy. They are going to recommend a Honda, regardless. Likewise, you should never work with an advisor whose company or affiliated company has proprietary funds. If you do, don't be surprised when they end up in your portfolio.

If you are working with a broker or dually registered advisor, take a look at your portfolio. Examine what you own. You will likely find that you are invested in some of the funds owned by the affiliated company. Ask yourself this: Are these the absolute best funds in the world for me? The answer is probably not. It is improbable that your advisor happens to work for the one company that has the absolute best investment for you for any allocation in your portfolio. It may happen at times, but it is not likely. If an advisor works for a company with its own funds or is affiliated with a company with its own funds, move on with your search.

A Final Thought on Conflicts

I have often heard people say that although they work with an advisor who has a conflict, it doesn't matter because their particular advisor is trustworthy, or they are always checking the advisor's advice. To those of you who feel this way, keep in mind that you might not be around one day. What sort of advice will your spouse or kids receive when you are gone? As an estate planning attorney, I have seen many instances of a surviving spouse being sold an annuity by an advisor before they even get to my office. You might also be around a long time but not have your wits about you for part of your life. When you and your family face the most challenging personal struggles, it's ideal to have a financial advisor who has no incentive to do anything differently. Warren Buffett is fond of saying he likes to buy a company that can be run by an idiot because one day it will be. I recommend always having an independent advisor who is not a broker because while the conflict of interest a broker brings to the table may not present itself today, one day it may.

Advisor Selection Issue #3—Competence

Never ascribe to malice that which adequately can be explained by incompetence.
—Napoleon Bonaparte

It's quite sad that we have eliminated most advisors simply because the overwhelming majority of them have a conflict of interest. They are salespeople, sometimes in bad disguises and other times in perfect disguises. We have now moved on to the thousands of independent advisors governed by the SEC, who are not also registered as brokers. While this group must act as a fiduciary at all times, they still need to be weeded out for competence and relevance.

The financial advisory field is quite different than other professions like medicine, law, engineering, education, and the like. If you want to be a doctor, you go to medical school. Lawyers go to law school. Engineers get a degree in engineering. Teachers get a degree in education. The overwhelming majority of financial advisors, I would speculate well over 95 percent, have no college education in financial planning or investment management because (until relatively recently) there wasn't a college-level program offered. They learn it on the job. Since that is the case, how do you identify an advisor with competence and relevance?

Competence Check #1—Do the Advisor's Credentials Meet Your Needs?

There are over 200 professional designations recognized on the FINRA website for the financial services industry. Most of them are worthless. If you are looking for financial planning help, be sure your advisor or someone on their team is a CERTIFIED FINANCIAL PLANNER™ practitioner (CFP®). If you are seeking advanced tax advice, get it from a CPA. If estate planning is required, utilize an estate planning attorney. These designations and degrees require a college degree, advanced studies, a formal exam, and continuing education. Set the bar at least at this level.

Competence Check #2—Is the Advisor Right for You?

An advisor can be an independent advisor with no conflicts, not have any proprietary funds, have the CFP®, and still not make sense for you. Be sure the advisor you choose works with people like you. If you are going to have heart surgery, you want to go to a doctor who successfully performs heart surgery all the time. If you are wrongfully accused of a crime,[6] you will look for a criminal defense attorney who has had prior success working with people in your situation. Likewise, when choosing a financial advisor, choose one who successfully works with people in your situation all the time. If you are just getting started, find an advisor who works primarily with clients at your life stage. If you have a high net worth, choose an advisor who works primarily with high-net-worth households. You don't want your advisor learning at the expense of your financial well-being. When an issue comes up, you want your advisor to have "been there, done that."

Competence Check #3—Is the Advisor Following a Process That You Agree With?

There are still thousands of independent advisors with no conflicts who don't sell proprietary funds and have experience with your type

---

[6]Or not wrongfully. I'm giving you the benefit of the doubt here!

of situation.[7] The final screen is to make sure that what they are selling actually works and fits your personal philosophy.

The financial services industry is a mess. Most advisors are not held to the highest legal standard of care. Most advisors are in the business of selling something, whether it is clear to the client or not. Even those who are genuinely independent may sell a strategy just because they know it's what people want to buy. It's easy for a financial advisor to sign on a client by telling the prospective client there is a way to participate in the upside of the market and at the same time get out of the way before a downturn. Whenever there is something people want to buy, someone will sell it. A competent and ethical advisor knows that this cannot be systemically done and won't sell it. A competent but unethical advisor knows it can't be done but will sell it anyway.

According to a recent study, an advisor following the principles outlined in this book can provide added value of about 3 percent per year, with some years adding negligible value and others adding value of well over 10 percent, notably during periods of large market swings (Kinniry, Jaconetti, DiJoseph, and Zilbering 2014). If the principles of this book ring true to you, then you should seek out an advisor who is focused on avoiding market timing, active trading, and selling performance, and instead is building a plan to develop a road map focused on an allocation that makes sense for you, keeping costs and taxes low, and following a disciplined, repeatable approach to investing that avoids behavioral missteps.

A Final Thought on Advisors—Principles

It's good to stand for something, believe in something, and base your business on values.

—Jerry Greenfield, Ben & Jerry's

Many advisors offer strategies like the one in this book but at the same time offer market timing strategies, tactical strategies, active trading, hedge funds, and the like. Select an advisor with principles and values. One who has something they believe in and implement for

---

[7]Though, sadly, the field is getting quite thin.

their clients, rather than a firm with a bunch of various "products and packages" trying to compete in every space. Suppose a firm offers an approach like the one outlined in this book but also offers a tactical strategy, downside protection strategy, or market timing strategy. In that case, they are telling you they will do anything to make a buck because they are selling strategies that directly contradict each other. It doesn't matter to them if something works or not. All that matters to them is selling you on becoming a client, no matter what strategy you want. You wouldn't choose a doctor who firmly believes in one approach to healing and believes another approach will actually harm you but would take that approach anyway.

If a prospective client comes to me looking for active options trading, equity hedge funds, market timing, and the like, I tell them I am not the advisor for them. I don't set up another fund to take them on. You should demand the same from an advisor. Once you determine the approach that's right for you, find an advisor who follows that approach as a matter of discipline and principle. Require that your advisor have conviction.

Avoiding Mistake #5—Choosing the Wrong Advisor

Be sure you put your feet in the right place, then stand firm.
                                                    —Abraham Lincoln

In my career, I have witnessed the unfortunate aftermath of many investment mistakes. It is always unfortunate when I see a client who blew up their portfolio. It is *tragic* when a financial advisor has caused the damage. I always feel the most sympathy for those who knew they needed help, sought it out, then ended up with an advisor who either put the client in commissionable products, sold them proprietary funds, caused them to miss out on gains because of a stupid market timing strategy, or blew up the portfolio with an active strategy.

A good list of questions to ask your advisor will include the following:

1. Where will my money be held? Right answer: Somewhere else!

2. Are you a broker? Right answer: No!

3. Are you a dually registered advisor? Right answer: No!

4. Do you or any affiliate sell proprietary investments of any kind? Right answer: No!

5. How are you compensated? Right answer: Total disclosure in writing and never make commissions on any investment product.

6. What are the credentials of you and your team? Right answer: If planning is involved, a CFP® is ideal to have on the team.

7. What is your planning and investment management approach? Right answer: The firm should follow a coherent philosophy rather than a bunch of different strategies (unprincipled) and should follow an approach that does not involve market timing or active trading.

If an advisor is the right solution for you, make your decision carefully. Understand the importance of custody and competence, but most importantly, *make sure your advisor has no conflict and follows the investment philosophy that makes sense for you.* Put your requirements in writing and stick to them. Do not be swayed in the meeting with a prospective advisor. Once you have put your feet in place, stand firm. A financial advisor can significantly increase the odds of you attaining your financial goals by providing peace of mind, offering continuity of advice for your family, partnering with you to make better financial decisions, and likely helping your portfolio perform better—that is, if you have the right advisor.

No Mistaking

Knowledge is knowing a tomato is a fruit. Wisdom is not putting it in a fruit salad.
—Miles Kington

When it comes to investing, much of the game is simply not messing things up. We have covered that in detail thus far. Of course, the goal is not only to avoid getting in the way of success; it is to maximize the odds of success.

Having gone over the key mistakes to avoid, we can move on to discuss how to optimize your results.

Rule #1: Have a Clearly Defined Plan

If you don't know where you are going, you'll end up someplace else.
—Yogi Berra

You don't start a race without knowing where the finish line is. You don't go on a hike without knowing your destination and the conditions you may encounter. You don't start driving somewhere without knowing where you are going.[1] Nonetheless, most investors invest without an endgame laid out in advance. Without a destination, it is easy to drift off course. Without a plan, it is easy to change the strategy midstream, increasing the odds of messing everything up.

Before you invest one dollar, you must have a plan. A plan does not need to be a 150-page road map of how you will invest every minute for the rest of your life. A plan can be very straightforward.

---

[1]My wife disputes this statement.

Step 1—Begin with determining the starting line, which is where you are today. Build a net worth statement that lays out all of your assets and liabilities.

Step 2—Know your goal. A goal must be very specific and realistic. An example of a goal that would not work well is: "I want to retire with a lot of money." Come on, people! We need to have a clearly defined purpose. Something like this will work: "I would like to retire at age 62 with an after-tax income of $100,000 per year, adjusted for inflation, and I want to assume Social Security will not be there for me." Now that is something we can work with!

Step 3—Run a projection showing how on track you are for that goal. There are online tools to help you do this, or your advisor can do this with you. Be sure to exclude assets that are not available to fund retirement. For example, if your net worth statement shows you have $800,000 today, but you plan to spend $150,000 on your kids' weddings and education, the projection should start with the money you have today that is available for retirement, which is $650,000 ($800,000 less the $150,000 you need for the kids). Then, include the money you are saving regularly, whether it is to your retirement plan at work, an IRA, or a taxable account reserved for retirement savings. These projections can get more sophisticated if you include Social Security, other income like pensions or rental income, potential inheritances, and other variables. Using these projections, we can determine how on track you may be for your goals.

Step 4—Determine if you need to adjust your goal. For example, if your projection shows that to hit your goal, you need to have an investment rate of return of 20 percent a year, well, change the goal because it very likely isn't going to work out. You can make adjustments by lowering your income need, saving more, pushing your retirement date out, or some combination of these.

Step 5—Move on to building the portfolio. Note that your plan needs to be revisited regularly (more on this later).

You may have different plans for different portfolios. For example, you may have separate investments set aside for education, which will have a different starting amount (what you have set aside) and a different goal (the amount of education you want to fund). You may have yet another goal for a second home, a wedding fund, or a trust set aside for kids or grandkids. Each of these portfolios should be constructed after a concrete plan has been laid out to clarify the objectives.

Finally, for those with excess wealth, which means having money beyond the pool of money you need to achieve all of your goals, it is acceptable to have the excess wealth portfolio's goal to simply "beat the S&P 500" or anything else you may fancy.[2] The key is to make sure that you have a solid portfolio in place to get you on track to financial security. After that, your excess wealth can be invested in a variety of ways.

In each case, whether it is for retirement, education, excess wealth, or any other portfolio, first determine a specific goal. Everything else flows from that purpose.

Rule #2: Avoid Asset Classes That Diminish Results

There are five major asset classes: cash, commodities (like gold and energy), stocks, bonds, and real estate. I will start with the two asset classes that should never be included in an investor's portfolio and then cover how to construct an allocation targeted toward your goals.

Cash—The Illusion of Safety

The one thing I will tell you is the worst investment you can have is cash. Everybody is talking about cash being king and all that sort of thing. Cash is going to become worth less over time. But good businesses are going to become worth more over time.

—Warren Buffett

---

[2] Note that we will cover how to do this later, and it won't include market timing, actively trading, or voodoo. (No offense to those of you who practice voodoo. It probably is more effective than market timing or actively trading stocks.)

When we think of risky asset classes, we tend to think of commodities, real estate, stocks, and even some bonds. Cash may be last on the list. Cash, however, has many inherent risks as well.

First and foremost, cash is the worst-performing asset class in history. Over long periods, cash has always underperformed all other major asset classes. The more time you spend with a significant portion of your holdings in cash, the higher the probability your portfolio will underperform.

Second, holding cash for long periods guarantees that you will not keep up with inflation. Cash guarantees the loss of purchasing power. In essence, your cash becomes worth less and less each year as prices go up, and your cash does not. Imagine you put $100,000 in the bank and earn 1 percent or so a year for ten years. When you pick up your cash, you may feel pretty good. However, the 1 percent or so you earned did not keep up with the cost of a stamp, a suit, a candy bar, health care, or education. You may think you made money, but you lost purchasing power.

One reason many "investors" hold cash is to time the market. They do this even though there has never been a documented, real-world study done by anyone showing that repeatedly moving from the market to cash and back to the market works. After all, you need to be right about when to get out, then when to get in, and do it over and over again. If you get burned just once, it can be "over," and your performance permanently affected.

Finally, many investors hold cash in the event of financial Armageddon, a situation when the stock market goes to zero or near zero and never recovers. In reality, if we live in a world where Walmart, Nike, McDonald's, Exxon Mobil, and the rest of the world's dominant companies go down and never recover, it will likely accompany a default by the U.S. government on treasury bonds. How can the U.S. government make its debt payments on its bonds if the major U.S. companies have collapsed? Who exactly would be working and paying taxes to cover the debt payments? In this event, cash is worthless as the FDIC guarantee would essentially mean nothing. If you do not believe America's largest corporations can survive, then the natural conclusion is that the U.S. economic system itself cannot survive. In that event, cash may be the worst asset to own.

Despite all of this, Americans are currently sitting on nearly $5 trillion in cash, surpassing the previous high set during the 2008 financial crisis. In typically tragic fashion, the peak of the move to cash in 2020 was the week of May 13, causing scores of investors to miss out on the subsequent 45% rebound in the markets.

Cash gives people comfort because, for goodness sake, it does not move around at all. It is easy to understand, and it does not "go down." But there is more to the story than that. While cash brings comfort, it does not keep up with inflation, continually loses purchasing power, drags down long-term investment returns, and is of no value in the event of an actual economic collapse. Keeping short-term reserves on hand is a good idea. Hoarding cash as a long-term investment—not so much. Eliminate cash as a consideration for your investment portfolio.

The Illusion of Gold as a Way to Grow Wealth

What motivates most gold purchasers is their belief that the ranks of the fearful will grow. During the past decade, that belief has proved correct. Beyond that, the rising price has on its own generated additional buying enthusiasm, attracting purchasers who see the rise as validating an investment thesis. As "bandwagon" investors join any party, they create their own truth—for a while.

—Warren Buffett[3]

In case you had not noticed, there is a gold rush taking place, with investors adding more and more of the precious metal to their portfolio.

---

[3]Also from Buffett, and much more entertaining: "Gold gets dug out of the ground in Africa, or someplace. Then we melt it down, dig another hole, bury it again, and pay people to stand around guarding it. It has no utility. Anyone watching from Mars would be scratching his head."

Many investors are flocking to gold as they worry that the dollar is losing so much value it may become worthless. Others worry the global economy will collapse, and gold will be the one real currency. Others view it as the safest place to be should we see high inflation.

Unlike companies, real estate, and other commodities (like energy), gold itself is nearly intrinsically worthless. Companies and real estate can create income. Energy companies have the potential to produce income. Oil itself is used as one of the most critical resources in the global economy. Gold produces no income and is not a critical resource. Historically, gold has performed worse than stocks, real estate, energy, and bonds, barely keeping pace with inflation (see Figure 6.1).

Every time in history it has outperformed substantially, it has ultimately collapsed. Finally, while gold has proven to underperform stocks and even bonds dramatically over the long run, it is still one of the most volatile asset classes. Gold belongs only in the portfolios of fearmongers and speculators. If you own gold in your portfolio, expect not to get paid an income, pay higher taxes on your returns, take a more volatile ride than the stock market, and get a long-term return lower than bonds. No thanks.

FIGURE 6.1

Source: Gold vs. Inflation, 2013. © AboutInflation.com.

Rule #3: Use Stocks and Bonds as the Core Building Blocks of Your Intelligently Constructed Portfolio

Bonds

Several studies have thoroughly documented that asset allocation is the primary driver of investment performance, accounting for 88 percent of a portfolio's returns. For example, if you own a handful of large-cap stocks, a large-cap mutual fund, or a large-cap index, you will get close to the same return most of the time. The other 12 percent of the portfolio's returns will be driven by other factors such as security selection and market timing, two factors that usually hurt performance.

Proper portfolio construction is part art, part science, and certainly never perfect, but it goes a long way toward following a plan that makes sense for your particular situation. Much is made of which asset classes are "good" or "bad" when in reality, it's your goals, not the various markets, that should drive the exposure to any given asset class in a portfolio. For most, but not all, investors, owning multiple asset classes to achieve various goals makes the most sense.

Bonds deliver a positive return about 85 percent of the time. With a bond, you are loaning money to a company or other entity. A treasury bond is a loan to the federal government; a municipal bond is a loan to a municipality such as a city or a state. A corporate bond is a loan to a corporation like McDonald's or Nike; a high-yield bond, also known as a junk bond, is a loan to a corporation that has to pay higher interest to attract investors to loan them money.

A lender is in a more predictable position than a stockholder. As long as the company stays around, the lender gets paid back with interest. A stockholder never really knows what will happen, as the stock can fluctuate all over the place. *It is for this reason that, over the long run, bonds are expected to underperform stocks. You should not own bonds on the expectation they will do otherwise.* So, if bonds are expected to underperform, why in the world might you buy them? Well, several reasons. First, while stocks are very likely to perform well over ten years, there is a lot of precedent for prolonged periods of misery (see 9/11, the tech bubble, or 2008/2009 for a modern-day refresher). Short-term income needs must be met for three to seven years so that the investor is never at the mercy of the stock market's often random gyrations. Between the bonds and your other income, you can cover your needs, whether or not there is a flash crash, someone flies into a building, a global pandemic, or any other event that occurs.

Basically, bonds are insurance. *We are giving up the expected return in exchange for dramatically increasing the likelihood the investor's needs will be met in the short and long run.* As an example, let's say you are retiring next year, and so long as you earn 6 percent per year, you will have the $120,000 per year you want in retirement. While stocks will likely outperform bonds throughout your retirement, we know two important things: (1) Stocks may underperform bonds in the first few years of your retirement, and (2) you don't need to be 100 percent in stocks to net a 6 percent return. Because of this, you should look at owning enough bonds to cover about five years of retirement to avoid the scenario of selling stock holdings during a bear market that may appear in the beginning stage of your golden years.

Finally, while much of this book is focused on the case for indexing your stock portfolio, the bond market is a different animal altogether. There is a fair debate about whether active management adds value in this space, so bond mutual funds, institutional funds, index funds, or individual bonds may be appropriate for your bond allocation.

Stocks

Stocks are the subject of ceaseless predictions when actually, they are the most unpredictable and, at the same time, predictable asset class. No one, absolutely no one, can predict the short-term movement of stock prices. As a reminder, anyone who tells you otherwise is likely an idiot or a liar (not sure which is worse, really). Yes, those are strong words, but with all the noise, it is vital to understand this as it impacts the allocation to this critical asset class. Because stocks are not predictable in the short run, investors should not own them to meet short-term needs. However, over the long run, stocks are expected to perform far better than bonds. Because stocks are riskier than bonds, they come with an implied "risk premium." If bonds were expected to perform as well as stocks, no one would ever take on the volatility that comes with owning stocks. Over the short run, stock prices are completely unpredictable. Yet over the long run, as a group, they have always done one thing: Go up—a lot.

While this inevitable outcome has persisted for over a century, the constant corrections, crashes, and day-to-day movements drive out the fainthearted or cause them to jump ship at the worst possible time. *Part of having the patience to make it through all this is to have stock market exposure only for the portion of your portfolio allocated for income needs more than five years out, depending on various factors.* If you are not at the mercy of the market over the next few years, and we know over the long run that the market has done nothing but go up, it becomes far easier to get through the rollercoaster ride along the way.

Suppose an investor has more than 10 to 20 years before part of the portfolio may be needed. In that case, this part can be invested in subsets of the market that are extremely volatile but have a long, well-documented history of rewarding the investor for their patience. Examples include mid-cap stocks, small-cap stocks, microcap stocks, and emerging markets stocks. The higher volatility should reward the investor with a higher return.

For example, if an investor has more than 20 years to retirement, they might have a substantial part of their portfolio in emerging markets. Some investors have wealth they will never spend or parts of the portfolio they will never touch. For situations like this, it can make sense for even a 75-year old to have a significant portion of their portfolio in small stocks or emerging markets stocks. However, *buyer beware!* If you cannot stand the heat, get the heck out of the kitchen. While on paper and over time, this strategy works well, it is not for the fainthearted. These sub-asset classes are often uncorrelated, can move quickly, and may underperform for long periods. *An excellent way to know if these sub-asset classes make sense for you is your reaction to a drop.* If you get excited at the opportunity to sell off bonds and buy more small caps and emerging markets while they are getting hammered, they will work well for you. If you find yourself generally freaking out about the drops, you will not last in the position long enough for it to work out, and you will cause your portfolio undue harm.

Alternative Investments

An entire book could be written on alternative investments.[4] In general, however, you can break them down into two camps: alternative ways to invest in public markets (like hedge funds) and investments that earn money outside of the public markets. Since I've already given you my perspective on hedge funds, I'll stick to the second type: investments outside of the public markets. Just as domestic companies tend to have an international counterpart (think Exxon and BP, Hershey's and Nestlé, etc.), public investments also have private counterparts. While you have stocks, bonds, and real estate in the public markets, you also have private equity, private lending, and private real estate. Let's take a quick look at each.

Private equity is owning shares of a company that isn't traded on the public exchanges. This may be either through the entrepreneur who owns the business or through one of the thousands of private equity firms that buy and sell shares in growing businesses. Investors in this space look to buy into or exit a firm at certain "stages." Venture capital investors are early-stage investors who may be putting money behind nothing more than an idea for a business with no existing product or revenues. Growth equity and buyout equity investors are later-stage investors looking to put money into a growing company to help scale the business to the point that it can be sold to another company or private equity investor or become publicly traded. A growth equity fund typically only has a minority ownership interest in the companies it invests in, meaning the business's day-to-day operational control remains with the original ownership team.

---

[4]Not one I would want to write, or you would want to read.

On the other hand, a buyout equity fund will typically buy a majority interest or even the entire company, giving them greater control over the operations of the business. Buyout funds also tend to employ leverage—which means they borrow money in addition to the capital they raise from investors—to purchase businesses. The fund managers use this strategy to maximize their financial resources and improve their return if their deals are profitable.

As we've already discussed, venture capital investing—despite the handful of "unicorn" companies who have enjoyed outsized success and made the space seem wildly more profitable than it is in reality—is almost always a sure path to underperformance. On the other hand, growth equity can have a place in a portfolio for higher-net-worth investors. Over the last 20 years, the data shows that growth equity firms have outperformed public markets consistently.

There are many reasons for this, but the short version is that successful growth equity firms can add significant value in scaling profitable businesses, which means their portfolio companies can increase in value by many multiples in a comparatively short period. For example, a restaurant owner who has built a successful business might have a couple of locations in one city. A growth equity firm can help reconfigure the business or service model so that the concept can be easily replicated in markets across the country. With the firm's help, the owner can open locations nationwide or franchise their operations. What was once a successful small business is now a major national brand, and the private equity investors reap the reward from the return on their investment.

This scenario is far removed from the many venture capital investments that often fail to survive or even make it to market. For example, look at Quibi, the short-form content mobile streaming app. Despite a litany of A-list celebrity and industry mogul involvement, the service shut down six months after launch, after having taken in nearly $2 billion in funding.[5]

---

[5]. . . and flushing it down the toilet.

Private lending can be thought of as an alternative to the public bond market. In this case, I'm primarily referring to middle-market lending funds. The idea behind these funds is to provide a source of capital to mid-sized businesses. If you are a business that needs to raise money, you can sell a portion of your company (typically to a private equity firm) or borrow money. Many private businesses find themselves too large to receive small business loans, too small for big bank loans, and unable to issue bonds in the public market. Middle-market lending funds fill that gap by providing loans to these businesses to fund operations or expansion. Like traditional loans, these may be secured (meaning they are backed by a piece of property, equipment, or other assets) or unsecured. Private lending has emerged as an asset class over the last ten years, so there's not enough history to guarantee these funds will outperform publicly traded bonds. However, based on the loan characteristics, the probability is reasonably high that these funds will deliver better risk-adjusted rates of return over time.

Private real estate can be broadly defined as any investment in real estate outside of publicly traded REITs. Some examples are a farmland lease, an apartment or office building, or even a rental property down the street. Much has been made of real estate as an asset class, primarily fueled by a narrative that it is somehow less risky than owning stocks. Every investment carries risk, including owning real estate; the risks are just different than owning stocks. Part of what makes real estate attractive as an investment is the use of leverage. Because most people finance the purchase of properties, a small amount of money can be used to buy a relatively large amount of real estate. The use of leverage also magnifies gains and losses. If you put 20% down on a property that increases 20% in value, you've made 100% profit; if instead, the property value goes down by 20%, you lose your entire investment if you're forced to sell. It's not uncommon to see real estate developers go bankrupt if their property portfolio ends up "underwater," where they have more debt than their properties are worth.

Private real estate funds exist to deploy investor capital into real estate projects. These funds may be pooled to construct a shopping center, hospital, or office building. Typically, the fund manager is looking to build the property, lease it to a tenant for a certain number of years, and then sell the development to someone else. These types of funds may be attractive to high-net-worth investors looking to add exposure to a specific type of real estate in their portfolio. Or the fund may be deploying capital into a project in economically disadvantaged areas—known as "opportunity zones"—that may qualify the investor for certain tax breaks.

History suggests that the types of private investments discussed here can outperform their public market counterparts. If you have the access, time, and resources to get the best-in-class offerings, exposure to these assets can improve the performance of your portfolio. However, these investments introduce certain complexities and complications as well. For example, to invest in many of these funds, you must meet minimum net worth or income thresholds to satisfy the legal requirements to be an investor. If you qualify, you can typically expect your investment funds to be tied up for at least 5–7 years before you can get your money back. These types of investments also increase the cost and complexity of preparing your tax return. Possibly most importantly, unlike investing in low-cost index funds—where history tells us the market is more likely to outperform active managers over time—with private funds, the experience, acumen, and execution of the manager is critical to the success of the fund. Having an experienced team to vet these opportunities and access to top-performing funds is essential for anyone interested in alternative investments.

Even if you meet all the requirements, investing in alternative assets isn't for everyone. For most investors, especially those who want to keep things low maintenance, a simple allocation of stocks and bonds can be far better than getting too cute with the portfolio. The goal is to increase the probability of achieving your goals. In the end, the wealth you have accumulated is a means to an end. You have some purpose for it. The asset classes and sub-asset classes you own should always be tied as closely as possible to your goals.

FIGURE 6.2	

Asset Allocation	1926–2012 Nominal Average Annual Returns
100% cash investments	3.60%
100% bonds	5.54%
80% bonds, 20% stocks	6.74%
70% bonds, 30% stocks	7.28%
60% bonds, 40% stocks	7.79%
50% bonds, 50% stocks	8.25%
40% bonds, 60% stocks	8.68%
30% bonds, 70% stocks	9.07%
20% bonds, 80% stocks	9.41%
100% stocks	9.97%

Source: Data from The Vanguard Group, Inc. 2013. "Vanguard's Principles for Investing Success."

Putting It All Together

The individual investor should act consistently as an investor and not as a speculator.

—Benjamin Graham

Knowing the rate of return required of the various portfolios, we can work our way to a basic allocation.

Looking at the returns, it seems to make sense to go "all in" with the stock market (see Figure 6.2).

Of course, nothing is that easy. The higher the allocation to stocks, the more volatile the portfolio will be. For example, a 100 percent stock portfolio has ranged from its best annual return of 54.2 percent to its worst at −43.1 percent. In comparison, a 60 percent stock/40 percent bond portfolio has ranged from a 36.7 percent best to a −26.6 percent worst return, a much narrower range of performance (see Figure 6.3).

Rule #4: Take a Global Approach

Investors tend to have a home country bias, meaning they invest most of their money in companies that operate from their home country. For example, Australians own a disproportionately large amount of their

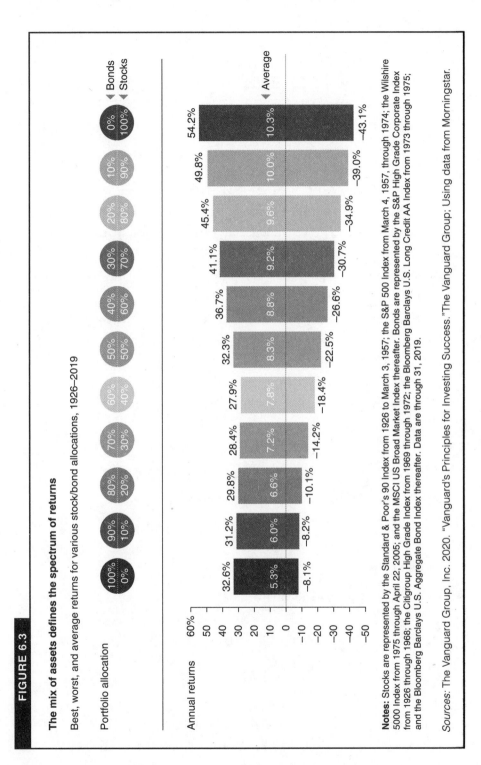

FIGURE 6.3

The mix of assets defines the spectrum of returns

Best, worst, and average returns for various stock/bond allocations, 1926–2019

Notes: Stocks are represented by the Standard & Poor's 90 Index from 1926 to March 3, 1957; the S&P 500 Index from March 4, 1957, through 1974; the Wilshire 5000 Index from 1975 through April 22, 2005; and the MSCI US Broad Market Index thereafter. Bonds are represented by the S&P High Grade Corporate Index from 1926 through 1968; the Citigroup High Grade Index from 1969 through 1972; the Bloomberg Barclays U.S. Long Credit AA Index from 1973 through 1975; and the Bloomberg Barclays U.S. Aggregate Bond Index thereafter. Data are through 31, 2019.

Sources: The Vanguard Group, Inc. 2020. "Vanguard's Principles for Investing Success." The Vanguard Group; Using data from Morningstar.

portfolio in home country stocks, as do investors throughout Europe and Asia. U.S. investors, more than any other country, can justify a home bias because there is a disproportionately large share of the global economy and stock market equity that are domiciled in the United States.

Nonetheless, U.S. investors should have international holdings as part of their portfolio for several reasons. First, we live in a global economy, and companies everywhere can and do make money. Second, international holdings often behave somewhat differently from U.S. holdings: the U.S. markets and international markets often "take turns" outperforming for short and sometimes long periods. This difference in returns can reduce portfolio volatility. Third, many international economies, especially the emerging market economies, have far higher projected growth rates than the United States.

One does not need to become an international exchange expert to create a global portfolio. By purchasing an index fund, an investor can instantly add global exposure. For example, if your allocation targets 60 percent stocks, you can assign 1/3 of that allocation to global stocks by buying an international ETF. The same can be done with your bond allocation.

Rule #5: Use Primarily Index-Based Positions

If the data do not prove that indexing wins, well, the data are wrong.

—John Bogle

As we covered in Chapter 2, actively trading securities in any asset class will likely yield lower returns. Choose index-based holdings for most if not all of your portfolio.

Rule #6: Don't Blow Out Your Existing Holdings

Know what you own and know why you own it.

—Peter Lynch

Once you have determined the right allocation for you, work toward it as quickly as possible. Any investments in tax-deferred accounts like

401(k)s, 403(b)s, IRAs, and the like can immediately be sold and repositioned. Any new money you add to the portfolio can be placed into the
new investments as well.

However, resist the temptation to sell all the holdings in your taxable account. While it is true that the S&P 500 will likely outperform
the large company stocks you currently own, it very likely may not
outperform on an after-tax basis. For example, if your target is to have
30 percent of your portfolio in large U.S. stocks, your holding for that
part of your portfolio is likely the S&P 500 index or a similar index.
Let's say you already own large U.S. companies like Microsoft, Walmart,
and ExxonMobil, and they have gained significant value. These capital
gains would be exposed to taxes if sold. Assuming they are not too large
a part of your portfolio, it makes sense to hold them and work around
them. For example, if those holdings are valued at $50,000 and $30,000
are gains, you could lose about one-quarter or more of the increase to
taxes if you sell. Instead, hold the positions and reduce the amount of
the S&P 500 you were going to purchase by the same amount. The goal
is to get as close as possible to the target portfolio without creating a tax
hit that likely cannot be overcome. Yes, the S&P 500 may do better, but
likely not by enough to cover the tax hit.

Another investment that may make sense to work around is an
annuity. While many annuities have very high expense ratios and limited investment options, it may make sense to hold them if surrender
charges are high. Wait to cash in until the surrender charges are zero or
low enough to be offset by the savings in the new portfolio. If you are
seriously ill, surrendering an annuity with a death benefit may not make
sense at all. In short, while other investments may be better, once you
have already purchased an annuity, there are many factors to take into
consideration before selling it.

There are also scenarios where I have advised clients to hold large
concentrated positions that make no sense to hold from a purely target-
portfolio perspective. For example, a new client had $3 million of their
$3.5 million net worth in one stock. They had hired my firm because
the husband was dying, and he wanted to be involved in choosing an

advisor to assist his wife when he was gone. I advised the couple to hold the security in the husband's name until his death. On his death, the stock received a step-up in basis. All the securities were sold without capital gains and repositioned into a new portfolio that made sense for her needs. Investing can at times be simple, but if tax or estate planning is involved, sometimes putting together a sound investment plan can do more harm than good due to the unintended consequences. Be aware of all the implications of portfolio repositioning before making changes.

Be wary of any advisor who recommends you "sell everything" regardless of tax consequences. It's irresponsible and lazy, and poor advice. Often, with customization, the portfolio can yield a far better after-tax result.

Rule #7: Be Sure You Can Live with Your Allocation

Know thyself.

—Socrates

I have three kids, and whenever we'd go to the amusement park when they were young, they'd examine the various rollercoasters. I could watch their minds at work. Some of the coasters are too boring for a 12-year-old, and some would get him excited. When he was younger, I would get a "maybe not this time" sort of look from him. Even kids attempt to make decisions as to the sort of ride they can handle.

In the past, I used to go on whatever rollercoaster they wanted. In recent years, I have often found that to be a regretful decision, particularly during the slow climb up some ridiculously high hill and the near vomit-inducing drop. Even then, though, I realize that getting off the rollercoaster and back on it in the middle of the ride is not a good idea. The odds are high that I will come out on the other end in one piece if I can follow it through to the end.

The markets are the same way.

The bond market is much like the kiddie coaster at Lego Land—almost anyone can handle it. The stock market is much like a big-time rollercoaster at Six Flags. The real estate market is like Space Mountain at Disney World: fast and in the dark. The commodity market is more like the Detonator: a ride that drops and lifts you unpredictably.

All of these rides have various levels of speed and volatility. Some find them thrilling; others find them nauseating. But in all cases, the rides generally reach a peaceful conclusion, even to the passengers who are wondering exactly what they just got themselves into.

The best time to evaluate the "rollercoaster" you are on is when the market is relatively stable. It is much easier to make that decision during a peaceful interlude than once the ride starts up again. And one day, it will definitely start up again.

This is easier said than done. Americans are great at forgetting things. It is a great coping mechanism that allows us to move on. After going on a rollercoaster with my son, I tell myself I won't do it again. But the next time I am at the amusement park with him, I agree to the stomach-dropping ride, not remembering how bad it felt the last time. Now, I no longer forget, and we make sure to take a friend of his along.

Smart investors customize their rollercoaster, taking parts of various markets to build a portfolio that meets their short-, intermediate-, and long-term needs. A portfolio can twist and turn, taking on the volatility necessary to meet the investor's specific goals. Still, it should be structured within the parameters that the investor is prepared to handle.

For many, the best portfolio is a portfolio that accomplished the intended goals with the least volatility possible. However, if the volatility is outside your bandwidth of tolerance, it is far better to adjust the goal or your savings plan than to make a mistake at the worst possible time.

Rule #8: Rebalance

If you do nothing else from here, your portfolio will probably work out fine. Still, you will likely end up taking more risk than you intended and paying more in taxes than required because you overlooked a key maintenance requirement: rebalancing your portfolio.

Rebalancing is a concept discussed a lot by advisors. Here is what you likely *won't* hear from most advisors: Rebalancing hurts your returns over the long run! And here is why: Over long periods of time, stocks outperform bonds. If you have a portfolio that is 60 percent stocks and 40 percent bonds, and you never rebalance, you may wake up 20 years from now with a portfolio that is 85 percent stocks and 15 percent bonds. There may be a scenario where it makes sense for you to have a more aggressive allocation 20 years from now than you have today, but it's unlikely. By rebalancing, you are intentionally keeping the portfolio aimed squarely at the target, thereby increasing the chances that you will hit your goal. It also increases the chances that you will not substantially underperform or outperform the goal.

Some investors rebalance periodically, such as every quarter or every year. I personally think that is overkill as it can often create unnecessary transactions and sometimes taxes. If a rebalance will create taxes or extensive transaction costs, consider skipping it unless your allocation is totally out of whack. On the other hand, if the market drops, don't wait! Take the opportunity to rebalance at that time, intentionally increasing your exposure to the weaker asset class, usually stocks, when they are down. If they keep going down, rebalance again! This is called opportunistic rebalancing and yields a better rate of return over time than periodic rebalancing. If this is just too much to deal with, simply confirm that your goals haven't changed and rebalance one to four times a year and get on with life!

Rule #9: Revisit the Plan

You don't need a parachute to skydive. You just need one to skydive twice.
                                        —Source unknown, author unknown

Revisit your plan and projections once a year or any time a significant change in your life occurs.[6] At your review, you will notice that your starting point may have changed. Your portfolio likely performed

---

[6] I am always fascinated by those who want to rerun their plan monthly or quarterly. This is overkill and goes precisely against a core premise of this book, which is to have a disciplined, long-term outlook, making adjustments as needed. If you are meeting with an advisor who is making changes based on a quarterly review or outlook, it's time to get a new advisor. If you are updating your own plan every week online, it is time to find a new hobby.

better or worse than expected over the previous year. You may have received an unexpected bonus, an inheritance, or had a liquidity event (for example, the sale of a property). The starting line has changed.

Perhaps your objectives are different now too. Maybe you want to retire sooner than you initially thought or are now going to work part-time in retirement. Perhaps the college your daughter wants to go to is twice as expensive as initially thought. Maybe the baby you were going to have ended up being triplets. Maybe now you are married, or newly single, or healthier, or more ill than expected. The finish line may have moved.

All sorts of things can change that should result in changes to the portfolio. Note that the emphasis on changes to the portfolio should be based more on personal changes than changes in various markets.

For example, let's say a 60-year-old investor has a goal of living on $100,000 per year at age 62. The projections used had assumed a portfolio rate of return of 6 percent, and she was right on track for her goal. At the review, the performance shows a return far better than projected due to a strong bull market, and the portfolio yielded 20 percent. The investor is also growing weary of portfolio volatility as she approaches retirement. Luckily for her, she no longer needs a 6 percent rate of return to accomplish her goals. The projections show a 5 percent rate of return is all she needs. Given these circumstances, the investor may pull back her exposure to stocks and increase her exposure to bonds. She would be doing this knowing full well that the expected long-term rate of return will be less, but the probability of getting the 5 percent will have increased with less volatility in the portfolio.

The Ultimate Rule: Don't Mess It Up!

As seen on CNBC:

Host: So, is this a buying opportunity?

Guest: *I wouldn't be a buyer of this market today (S&P at 1,740), but I would be a huge buyer at S&P 1,725.*

This CNBC interaction illustrates precisely the wrong way to look at your portfolio. How can an allocation to stocks make no sense for an investor at S&P 1,740 but a lot of sense at 1,725?! Once you have the portfolio in place, *stay disciplined*. Follow the pattern of investment decisions outlined in this chapter or work with an advisor who understands, accepts, and invests with these principles. Ignore the noise, never panic, don't change plans in the middle of a crisis, and stay focused on your goals.

Portfolio Example

Common sense attests that some people can and do beat the market. It's not all chance. Many academics agree, but the method of beating the market, they say, is not to exercise superior clairvoyance but rather to assume greater risk. Risk, and risk alone, determines the degree to which returns will be above or below average.
—Burton G. Malkiel, *A Random Walk Down Wall Street*

The "I Want to Beat the Market" Portfolio

This book explains why you can't beat the market by market timing or actively trading stocks. If you want to beat the market and define the market as the S&P 500, then the way to beat it over time is to increase the portfolio's exposure to asset classes that are likely to outperform large-cap U.S. stocks over long periods. Examples of such riskier asset classes are small U.S. stocks and emerging markets stocks. A "beat the market" portfolio may look like the one shown in Figure 6.4.

The "I Need 7 Percent to Hit My Long-Term Retirement Goal" Portfolio

A portfolio diversified across various asset classes and with a global approach has a reasonable probability of achieving the returns the typical investor requires. Such a portfolio may look like the one shown in Figure 6.5. Small-cap stocks tend to pull up returns over the long run, but the cost is long periods of underperformance. The U.S. tends to outperform or underperform international stocks, often for long periods. Keep this in mind during the rough periods!

FIGURE 6.4

"I Want to Beat the Market" Portfolio

FIGURE 6.5

"I Need 7 Percent to Hit My Long-Term Goal" Portfolio

The "Get Me What I Need for the Rest of My Life with the Least Volatility Possible" Portfolio

This portfolio should have enough stocks to pull the rate of return to where it needs to be over a long period, but enough bonds to allow the

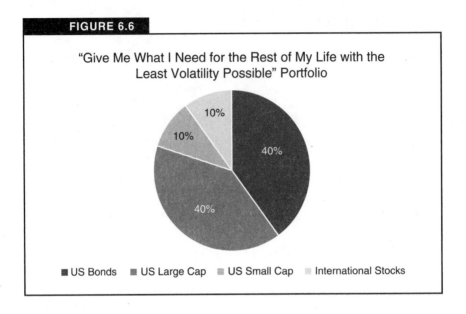

FIGURE 6.6

"Give Me What I Need for the Rest of My Life with the Least Volatility Possible" Portfolio

■ US Bonds   ■ US Large Cap   ■ US Small Cap   ▨ International Stocks

investor to take monthly or annual distributions without selling stocks in a down market. For an investor with $1,000,000 and who needs $50,000 per year, the portfolio may look like the one shown in Figure 6.6.

The "I Have More Money Than I Will Ever Need and I Want It to Grow with Minimal Volatility" Portfolio

This portfolio is for someone who has enough money that the income alone from stocks and bonds will meet their needs for life, even when adjusted for inflation. Despite reading this book, this person is fearful of stocks and wants a low-volatility portfolio that will allow her to draw about 3 percent without invading the principal (see Figure 6.7).

The "I Have More Money Than I Will Ever Need, Volatility Doesn't Bother Me, and I Want It to Grow Along with the Market" Portfolio

Some people are fortunate enough to have more investable assets than they could ever possibly spend. A subset of this group is not bothered by volatility, accepts that stocks will likely outperform bonds, and wants to

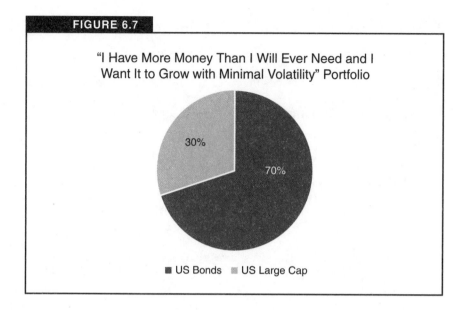

FIGURE 6.7

"I Have More Money Than I Will Ever Need and I Want It to Grow with Minimal Volatility" Portfolio

30%

70%

■ US Bonds ■ US Large Cap

participate in the market return, all without taking significant excess risk to try to beat the market return. For this group, a portfolio might look like the one shown in Figure 6.8.

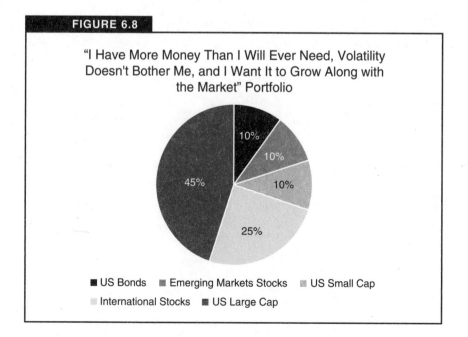

FIGURE 6.8

"I Have More Money Than I Will Ever Need, Volatility Doesn't Bother Me, and I Want It to Grow Along with the Market" Portfolio

10%

10%

10%

45%

25%

■ US Bonds ■ Emerging Markets Stocks ■ US Small Cap
■ International Stocks ■ US Large Cap

A Path to Success: Intelligent Portfolio Construction

Some of the principles of portfolio construction are very straightforward:

- Avoid market timing; instead, invest for the long run.
- Avoid active trading; buy mostly passive investments.
- Don't fall for performance claims, get scared by the media, and the like; tune out the noise.
- Don't get in your own way; be aware of your behavioral biases, recognize them when they appear, and control them.
- Build a portfolio with asset classes that make sense for your situation.

For some, especially higher-net-worth investors, the portfolio construction can get more sophisticated. To match yourself to a portfolio that will not only accomplish your goals but that you can also live with, measure the return you need against the volatility you can handle. For good measure, make sure you consider taxes, as well as changing circumstances. While the portfolio itself should not be highly active, you must put more into it than simply choosing a few indexes and leaving it at that!

You're the One

Life is what happens while you are busy making other plans.

—John Lennon

In 1970, a prominent politician offered my dad, his physician, some free advice. "Alex," he said, "I have all the money in the world, but I never enjoyed it. Make time to enjoy yourself." My dad took the advice to heart and expanded his vacation schedule.

I have observed the wisdom in this advice throughout my career. While I lead an investment committee, I am also a wealth manager and estate planning attorney, and I help clients formulate and take action on their financial plans. My firm regularly works with clients throughout their lives, through incapacity, and with their families on death. Many of these very successful people have done a great job of saving a fair amount of wealth and somehow never messing things up along the way. These are two very difficult things to achieve. I have seen that these people certainly don't deprive themselves, but they are not enjoying their position to their fullest. Many of these folks got where they are by being thrifty and diligent. It is not uncommon for a client to save in their IRA every year for their entire life. When they turn 72, and the government forces a withdrawal, they ask me how to avoid taking the money out. They have been putting money in for so long, and they can't bear the thought of spending it!

Let me tell you something about your money.

It makes no difference whether your heirs inherit $250,000 instead of $300,000, $600,000 instead of $800,000, $1.2 million instead of $1.4 million, or $10 million instead of $11 million; enjoy yourself and the wealth you have spent your life creating and preserving.

After preparing a net worth statement with a client, he said to me, "I would like to die and come back as my kids."

Your estate at death isn't just your investment account. It is also the value of your home, insurance, cars, and so on. It will all likely be liquidated, thrown into a pot, and split up.

If you are financially independent, let me contradict just about everything you hear from financial advisors when I tell you to get that extra-tall cup of expensive coffee, quit driving that 10-year-old car,[1] and upgrade your next vacation. Believe me when I tell you that your kids will! I have seen kids buy new cars and homes within days of receiving an inheritance.

If you are charitably inclined and financially independent, go ahead and experience the pleasure of giving now. *Enjoy it!* Why wait until you are dead? If you insist on passing your wealth to your kids at your own expense, go ahead and do it now. Enjoy passing the wealth onto your kids and grandkids rather than them receiving larger checks when you are no longer around. The bottom line is this: *It's your money.* You busted your butt for it, you saved it, and you preserved it. So long as you are not jeopardizing your financial security, enjoy yourself a bit, give away what you want too, and overall, loosen up a bit and experience the fruits of your labor.

---

[1] Seriously, get a new car! You know, one with current technology and safety features! If it's 10 years old, you aren't even protecting yourself. This is your life we are talking about here! You don't use a 10-year-old computer, do you? Oh my goodness! If you do, get a new computer too! Geez!!

Let's Roll!!

Simple can be harder than complex. You have to work hard to get your thinking clean to make it simple.

— Steve Jobs

From Steve Jobs, Former CEO of Apple Inc. © Steve Jobs

Market timing, active trading, acting on bad information, making behavioral mistakes, or hiring the wrong advisor can all lead to the permanent damage of your financial well-being. Being aware of these critical pitfalls is the best way to recognize and avoid them. You can do better than that, though!

By following the guidelines on how best to manage your wealth, you can not only avoid the mistakes but optimize your wealth. If an advisor is the best fit for you, demand one who follows these principles, and you can enjoy life knowing you are following a path to success.

Reading this is one thing; acting on it is another. Financial advisors and financial media are actively working to suck you back into methods that sound good but don't work. Resist the urge to fall prey to their temptations. You know how to do this. Don't let anyone tell you that the system isn't complicated enough or sexy enough. That's a bunch of hooey. With investing, the less clutter, the better.

With discipline, you and your advisor can follow this system through all kinds of markets, and most importantly, stick with it through down markets. You will be financially and emotionally better off for it!

Keep in mind that it is not enough to follow the system some of the time. Nothing will happen if you eat a donut for breakfast, cake for lunch, and ice cream for dinner. But if you do it every day for a few years, you will be dead. If you text and drive once, it might turn out just fine. If you do it all the time, eventually, you are likely to crash. The key to successful investing is to focus on repeatable behavior using a disciplined, ongoing system. Take what you have learned, develop a plan of action, and stick to the plan. You can do this. Let's roll![1]

The best time to plant a tree was yesterday. The second-best time is today.
— *Chinese Proverb*[2]

---

[1] I mean like right now! Let's roll! Quit putting it off. Get a plan together and get on the right track today!

[2] While Americans say macho things like, "Let's roll," the Chinese came up with a much more eloquent way to say the same thing!

References

AboutInflation.com. 2013. "Gold vs. Inflation." Retrieved from www.aboutinflation .com/gold-vs-inflation.

Alpert, Marc, and Howard Raiffa. 1982. "A Progress Report on the Training of Probability Assessors." In *Judgment Under Uncertainty: Heuristics and Biases*, edited by Daniel Kahneman, Paul Slovic, and Amos Tversky, 294–305. Cambridge: Cambridge University Press.

Amabile, Teresa M., and Steven J. Kramer. 2011. "The Power of Small Wins." *Harvard Business Review* 89 (5): 70–80.

Arkes, Hal R., Cynthia A. Joyner, Mark V. Pezzo, Jane Gradwohl Nash, Karen Siegel-Jacobs, and Eric Stone. 1994. "The Psychology of Windfall Gains." *Organizational Behavior and Human Decision Processes* 59:331–347.

Armor, David A., and Shelley E. Taylor. 2002. "When Predictions Fail: The Dilemma of Unrealistic Optimism." In *Heuristics and Biases: The Psychology of Intuitive Judgment*, edited by Thomas Gilovich, Dale Griffin, and Daniel Kahneman, 334–348. Cambridge: Cambridge University Press.

Arnold, Tom, John H. Earl, and David S. North. 2007. "Are Cover Stories Effective Contrarian Indicators?" *Financial Analysts Journal* 63 (2): 70–75.

Averill, James R. 1980. "A Constructivist View of Emotion." In *Emotion: Theory, Research and Experience 1*, edited by R. Plutchik and H. Kellerman, 305–339. New York: Academic Press.

"Guide to the Markets, U.S. 4Q 2020, As of September 30, 2020," Samantha M. Azzarello, Jordan K. Jackson, David M. Lebovitz, Jennie Li, John C. Manley, Meera Pandit, Gabriela D. Santos, and David P. Kelly, https://am.jpmorgan.com/blobgim/1383407651970/83456/MI-GTM-4Q20.pdf. Retrieved10/4/2020.

Barber, Brad M., and Terrance Odean. 2001. "Boys Will Be Boys: Gender, Overconfidence, and Common Stock Investment." *The Quarterly Journal of Economics* 116 (1, February): 261–292.

Barrett, Amy L., and Brent R. Brodeski. 2006. "Survivor Bias and Improper Measurements: How the Mutual Fund Industry Inflates Actively Managed Fund Performance." Zero Alpha Group and Savant Capital Management, Inc. Retrieved from www.etf.com/docs/sbiasstudy.pdf?iu=1.

Bauer, Richard J., and Julie R. Dahlquist. 2001. "Market Timing and Roulette Wheels." *Financial Analysts Journal* 57 (1, January–February): 28–40.

Bespoke Investment Group. 2012. "Wall Street Strategists Remain Bearish." Retrieved from www.bespokeinvest.com/thinkbig/2012/3/12/wall-street-strategists-remain-bearish.html.

Britton, Diana. 2011. "Is Tactical Investing Wall Street's Next Clown Act?" WealthManagement.com. Retrieved from http://wealthmanagement.com/investment/tactical-investing-wall-streets-next-clown-act.

Christensen-Szalanski, Jay J., and James B. Bushyhead. 1981. "Physicians' Use of Probabilistic Information in a Real Clinical Setting." *Journal of Experimental Psychology: Human Perception and Performance* 7 (4, August): 928–935.

Cowles, A. 3rd. 1933. "Can Stock Market Forecasters Forecast?" *Econometrics* 1 (2, April): 309–324.

Crary, David. 2008. "Students Lie, Cheat, Steal, But Say They're Good." Associated Press, November 30.

Cross, K. Patricia. 1977. "Not Can, But *Will* College Teaching Be Improved?" *New Directions for Higher Education* 17:1–15.

CXO Advisory Group, LLC. 2013. "'Sell in May' Over the Long Run." Retrieved from www.cxoadvisory.com/3873/calendar-effects/sell-in-may-over-the-long-run/.

Daniel, Kent, David Hirshleifer, and Avanidhar Subrahmanyam. 1998. "Investor Psychology and Security Market Under-and Overreactions." *Journal of Finance* 53 (6): 1839–1885.

Denrell, Jerker, and Christina Fang. 2010. "Predicting the Next Big Thing: Success as a Signal of Poor Judgment." *Management Science* 56 (10): 1653–1667.

Dent, Harry S. Jr. 2006. *The Next Great Bubble Boom: How to Profit from the Greatest Boom in History: 2006–2010.* New York: Free Press.

Dent, Harry S. Jr. 2008. *The Great Depression Ahead: How to Prosper in the Crash Following the Greatest Boom in History.* New York: Free Press.

Dent, Harry. 2013. "Survive and Prosper." Retrieved from http://survive-prosper.com/pages/latest-research/landing/google/N704-PPC-Winter-Dow-Today-3300-CN.php?code=X195N704.

NYT Roubini Article, IMF Transcript. Economic Cycle Research Institute. Retrieved from https://www.businesscycle.com/ecri-news-events/news-details/nyt-roubini-article-imf-transcript.

Ellis, Charles D. 2012. "Murder on the Orient Express: The Mystery of Underperformance." *Financial Analysts Journal* 68 (4, July–August): 13–19.

Ferri, Rick. 2013. "Busting the Sell in May and Go Away Myth." *Forbes*, April 8. Retrieved from www.forbes.com/sites/rickferri/2013/04/08/busting-the-sell-in-may-and-go-away-myth/.

Fidelity Viewpoints. 2013. "Get Ready for the Next Market Crisis." Fidelity Investments. Retrieved from https://www.fidelity.com/viewpoints/investing-ideas/get-ready-for-the-next-crisis.

Fisher Investments. "How We're Different." Retrieved from www.fisherinvestments.com/en-us/about/fisher-difference.

Fisher, Ken. 2007. "The Fall 2007 Rally." *Forbes*, September 17. Retrieved from www.forbes.com/free_forbes/2007/0917/210.html.

Fisher, Ken. 2008. "We're Too Gloomy." *Forbes*, January 28.

Fox, Justin. 2014. "What Alan Greenspan Has Learned Since 2008." *The Harvard Business Review Blog Network*. Retrieved from http://blogs.hbr.org/2014/01/what-alan-greenspan-has-learned-since-2008/.

Grable, John E., and Sonya L. Britt. 2012. "Financial News and Client Stress: Understanding the Association from a Financial Planning Perspective." Kansas State University Financial Planning Research Center.

Graham, John R., and Campbell R. Harvey. 1994. "Market Timing Ability and Volatility Implied in Investment Newsletters' Asset Allocation Recommendations." Fuqua School of Business, Duke University.

"Ken Fisher profile," Gurufocus.com, . 2020. "Ken Fisher Profile." https://www.gurufocus.com/guru/ken+fisher/profile.

Haizlip, Julie, Natalie May, John Schorling, Anne Williams, and Margaret Plews-Ogan. 2012. "Perspective: The Negativity Bias, Medical Education, and the Culture of Academic Medicine: Why Culture Change Is Hard." *Academic Medicine* 87 (9, September): 1205–1209.

Hamlin, J. Kiley, Karen Wynn, and Paul Bloom. 2010. "Three-Month-Olds Show a Negativity Bias in Their Social Evaluations." *Developmental Science* 13 (6): 923–929.

Hartung, Adam. 2012. "Want a Better Economy? History Says Vote Democrat!" *Forbes*, October 10. Retrieved from www.forbes.com/sites/adamhartung/2012/10/10/want-a-better-economy-history-says-vote-democrat/.

Heuer, Richard J. Jr. 1999. *Psychology of Intelligence Analysis*. Washington, DC: Center for the Study of Intelligence, Central Intelligence Agency.

Housel, Morgan. 2014. "The World's Smartest Investors Have Failed." *The Motley Fool*. Retrieved from www.fool.com/investing/general/2014/01/27/the-worlds-smartest-investors-have-failed.aspx.

Israelsen, Craig L. 2010. "What's in a Name?" *Financial Planning*, June 1.

"Here's what you likely have in common with Harvard's endowment managers," Mark Hulbert. Marketwatch.com. https://www.marketwatch.com/story/heres-what-you-likely-have-in-common-with-harvards-endowment-managers-2019-10-08. Retrieved 10/4/2020.

Jeffrey, Robert H. 1984. "The Folly of Stock Market Timing." *Harvard Business Review* (July–August): 102–110.

Kahneman, Daniel, and Amos Tversky. 1984. "Choices, Values, and Frames." *The American Psychologist* 39 (4): 341–350.

Kahneman, Daniel, and Dan Lovallo. 1993. "Timid Choices and Bold Forecasts: A Cognitive Perspective on Risk Taking." *Management Science* 39 (1): 17–31.

Kahneman, Daniel, Jack L. Knetsch, and Richard H. Thaler. 1991. "Anomalies: The Endowment Effect, Loss Aversion, and Status Quo Bias." *Journal of Economic Perspectives* 5 (1): 193–206.

Kinniry, Francis M. Jr., Colleen M. Jaconetti, Michael A. DiJoseph, and Yan Zilbering. 2014. "Putting a Value on Your Value: Quantifying Vanguard Advisor's Alpha." The Vanguard Group, Inc. Retrieved from https://advisors.vanguard.com/iwe/pdf/ISGQVAA.pdf?cbdForceDomain=true.

Kopecki, Dawn, Clea Benson, and Phil Mattingly. 2012. "Dimon Says Overconfidence Fueled Loss He Can't Defend." *Bloomberg*. Retrieved from www.bloomberg.com/news/2012-06-14/dimon-says—overconfidencefueled-loss-he-can-t-defend.html.

Lauricella, Tom. 2005. "Yale Manager Blasts Industry; His Advice to Individuals: Choose Index Funds, ETFs Over Active Managers." *Wall Street Journal Online*. Retrieved from http://online.wsj.com/news/articles/SB112597100191832366.

Marano, Hara Estroff. 2004. "Marriage Math." Psychology Today, March 16. Retrieved from www.psychologytoday.com/articles/200403/marriage-math.

Marquet, Christopher T. 2011. "The Marquet Report on Ponzi Schemes." Marquet International, Ltd. Retrieved from www.marquetinternational.com/pdf/marquet_report_on_ponzi_schemes.pdf.

McCall, Tommy. 2008. "Bulls, Bears, Donkeys and Elephants." *New York Times*, October 14. Retrieved from www.nytimes.com/interactive/2008/10/14/opinion/20081014_OPCHART.html?_r=0.

McElroy, Todd, and Keith Dowd. 2007. "Susceptibility to Anchoring Effects: How Openness-to-Experience Influences Responses to Anchoring Cues." *Judgment and Decision Making* 2 (1, February): 48–53.

Montier, James. 2006. *Behaving Badly*. London: Dresdner Kleinwort Wasserstein Securities.

Mulcahy, Diane, Bill Weeks, and Harold S. Bradley. 2012. "We Have Met the Enemy . . . and He Is Us: Lessons from Twenty Years of the Kauffman Foundation's Investments in Venture Capital Funds and the Triumph of Hope Over Experience." Ewing Marion Kauffman Foundation. Retrieved from www.kauffman.org/~/media/kauffman_org/research%20reports%20and%20covers/2012/05/we%20have%20met%20the%20enemy%20and%20he%20is%20us(1).pdf.

"S&P 500 P/E Ratio by Year," multpl.com. https://www.multpl.com/s-p-500-pe-ratio/table/by-year. Retrieved 10/4/2020.

"Fund Outflows in March Topped Outflows in October 2008," Bernice Napach, Thinkadvisor.com. https://www.thinkadvisor.com/2020/04/20/fund-outflows-in-march-topped-outflows-inoctober-2008/. Retrieved 10/4/2020.

The National Association of Personal Financial Planners. *Pursuit of a Financial Advisor: Field Guide*. Arlington Heights, IL: National Association of Personal Financial Planners. Retrieved from www.napfa.org/UserFiles/File/FinancialAdvisorFieldGuidev13.pdf.

Odean, Terrance. 1998. "Volume, Volatility, Price, and Profit When All Traders Are Above Average." *Journal of Finance* 53 (6): 1887–1934.

Park, Jae Hong, Prabhudev Konana, Bin Gu, Alok Kumar, and Rajagopal Raghunathan. 2010. "Confirmation Bias, Overconfidence, and Investment Performance: Evidence from Stock Message Boards." McCombs Research Paper Series No. IROM-07-10. Retrieved from http://ssrn.com/abstract=1639470.

Patel, Sital S. 2013. "Madoff: Don't Let Wall Street Scam You, Like I Did." *MarketWatch*. Retrieved from www.marketwatch.com/story/madoff-dont-let-wall-street-scam-you-like-i-did-2013-06-05?pagenumber=2.

PBS's *Frontline*. 2013. "The Retirement Gamble." [JW Player video file.] Retrieved from www.pbs.org/wgbh/pages/frontline/retirement-gamble/.

Peter Schiff Predictions. Wall Street Economists Institute. Retrieved from http://economicpredictions.org/peter-schiff-predictions/index.htm.

Philips, Christopher B., Francis M. Kinniry, Jr., and Todd Schlanger. 2013. "The Case for Index-Fund Investing." The Vanguard Group, Inc. Retrieved from https://personal.vanguard.com/pdf/s296.pdf.

"Active fund managers trail the S&P 500 for the ninth year in a row in a triumph for indexing," Bob Pisani, CNBC.com. https://www.cnbc.com/2019/03/15/active-fund-managers-trail-the-sp-500-for-the-ninth-year-in-a-row-in-triumph-for-indexing.html.Retrieved 10/7/2020.

Plous, Scott. 1993. *The Psychology of Judgment and Decision Making*. New York: McGraw-Hill.

Ptak, Jeffrey. 2012. "In Practice: Tactical Funds Miss Their Chance." *Morningstar Advisor*. Retrieved from http://advisors.morningstar.com/advisor/t/51504278/in-practice-tactical-funds-miss-their-chance.htm?&q=tactical&single=true.

Riepe, Mark W. 2013. "Does Market Timing Work?" Charles Schwab. Retrieved from www.schwab.com/public/schwab/nn/articles/Does-Market-Timing-Work.

Roth, Allan. 2012. "Second Dent Investment Fund to Disappear." *CBS Money Watch*. Retrieved from www.cbsnews.com/news/second-dent-investment-fund-to-disappear/.

"Endowment Returns Solid in 2019", Rick Seltzer. Insidehighered.com. https://www.insidehighered.com/news/2020/01/30/endowment-returns-10-year-average-rises-leaders-see-cloudshorizon. Retrieved 10/7/2020.

Sharpe, William F. 1975. "Likely Gains from Market Timing." *Financial Analysts Journal* 31 (2): 60–69.

Shtekhman, Anatoly, Christos Tasopoulos, and Brian Wimmer. 2012. "Dollar-Cost Averaging Just Means Taking Risk Later." The Vanguard Group, Inc. Retrieved from https://institutional.vanguard.com/iam/pdf/ICRDCA.pdf?cbdForceDomain=true.

Slovic, Paul. 1973. "Behavioral Problems of Adhering to a Decision Policy." Paper presented at the Institute for Quantitative Research in Finance, May 1, Napa, California.

Snider, Kim. 2014. "The Great Market Timing Lie." Snider Advisors. Retrieved from https://www.snideradvisors.com/KimSnider/Web/FreeStuff/Market-Timing.aspx.

S&P Dow Jones Indices, LLC. 2014. "S&P Dow Jones Indices." McGraw Hill Financial. Retrieved from www.djindexes.com/.

Sullivan, Todd. 2008. "Being Wrong for Five Years Makes Peter Schiff Right Now?" Seeking Alpha. Retrieved from http://seekingalpha.com/article/106824-being-wrong-for-five-years-makes-peter-schiff-right-now.

Sumner, Mark. 2008. "Whither Goest Thou, Stock Market?" Kos Media, LLC. Retrieved from www.dailykos.com/story/2008/12/02/668445/-Whither-Goest-Thou-Stock-Market#.

Svenson, Ola. 1981. "Are We All Less Risky and More Skillful Than Our Fellow Drivers?" *Acta Psychologica* 47 (2): 143–148.

Taleb, Nassim Nicholas. 2007. *The Black Swan.* New York: Random House.

Tottenham, Nim, Jessica Phuong, Jessica Flannery, Laurel Gabard-Durnam, and Bonnie Goff. 2013. "A Negativity Bias for Ambiguous Facial-Expression Valence during Childhood: Converging Evidence from Behavior and Facial Corrugator Muscle Responses." *Emotion* 13 (1): 92–103.

Van Eaton, R. Douglas. 2000. "The Psychology Behind Common Investor Mistakes." *American Association of Individual Investors Journal* 22 (April): 2–5.

The Vanguard Group, Inc. 2013a. "Tax Efficiency: A Decisive Advantage for Index Funds." Retrieved from https://advisors.vanguard.com/VGApp/iip/site/advisor/researchcommentary/article/IWE_InvComTaxEfficiency.

The Vanguard Group, Inc. 2013b. "Vanguard's Principles for Investing Success." Retrieved from https://personal.vanguard.com/pdf/s700.pdf.

"Vanguard's Principles for Investing Success," The Vanguard Group, Inc. Vanguard.com, https://about.vanguard.com/what-sets-vanguard-apart/principles-for-investingsuccess/ ISGPRINC_062020_Online.pdf, Page 10. Retrieved 10/4/2020.

Vardi, Nathan. 2012. "Billionaire John Paulson's Hedge Fund: Too Big to Manage." *Forbes*, December 21.

Voigt, Kevin. 2011. "October: The Scariest Month for Stocks?" CNN. Retrieved from http://business.blogs.cnn.com/2011/10/04/october-the-scariest-month-for-stocks/.

Wagenaar, Willem, and Gideon B. Keren. 1986. "Does the Expert Know? The Reliability of Predictions and Confidence Ratings of Experts." In *Intelligent Decision Support in Process Environments*, edited by Erik Hollnagel, Giuseppe Mancini, and David D. Woods, 87–103. Berlin: Springer.

Waggoner, John. 2005. "Top-Selling Funds of 2000 in Deep Red." *USA Today*, April 5.

Wallick, Daniel W., Brian R. Wimmer, and Todd Schlanger. 2012. "Assessing Endowment Performance: The Enduring Role of Low-Cost Investing." The Vanguard Group, Inc. Retrieved from https://institutional.vanguard .com/iam/pdf/ICR25P.pdf?cbdForceDomain=true.

Wansink, Brian, Robert J. Kent, and Stephen J. Hoch. 1998. "An Anchoring and Adjustment Model of Purchase Quantity Decisions." *Journal of Marketing Research* 35 (February): 71–81.

Weber, Tim. 2011. "Davos 2011: Why Do Economists Get It So Wrong?" BBC. Retrieved from www.bbc.co.uk/news/business-12294332.

Willoughby, Jack. 2010. "Lifting Beyond Their Weight Class." *Barron's*, July 10.

Wimmer, Brian R., Sandeep S. Chhabra, and Daniel W. Wallick. 2013. "The Bumpy Road to Outperformance." The Vanguard Group, Inc. Retrieved from https://institutional.vanguard.com/iam/pdf/outper-formance_research_paper.pdf?cbdForceDomain=true.

Nouriel Roubini Predictions. Wall Street Economists Institute. Retrieved from http://economicpredictions.org/nouriel-roubini-predictions.index.htm

"Listed domestic companies, total – United States," The World Bank, https:// data.worldbank.org/indicator/CM.MKT.LDOM. NO?locations=US. Retrieved 10/7/2020.

Young, David. 2007. "To Succeed, Keep It Simple." *Investment Advisor*, February 1.

Zacharakis, Andrew, and Dean Shepherd. 2001. "The Nature of Information and Overconfidence on Venture Capitalists' Decision Making." *Journal of Business Venturing*, 16 (4): 311–332.

Zelizer, Viviana A. 1994. *The Social Meaning of Money: Pin Money, Paychecks, Poor Relief, and Other Currencies*. New York: Basic Books.

Index

Page numbers followed by *f* refer to figures.